Practical Yacht Handling

Practical Yacht Handling

Eric Tabarly

Illustrations by Antoine Lamazou
Translated by Mark Brackenbury

STANFORD MARITIME · LONDON

Stanford Maritime Limited
Member Company of the George Philip Group
12–14 Long Acre   London WC2E 9LP
Editor Phoebe Mason

Originally published as *Guide Pratique de Manœuvre*
Copyright © Editions du Pen Duick, Paris 1978

First published in Great Britain 1980
English translation © Stanford Maritime Limited 1980
Translated by Mark Brackenbury

Set in Monophoto 12/14 Times
Printed in Great Britain by
Butler & Tanner Ltd,
Frome and London

British Library Cataloguing in Publication Data
Tabarly, Eric
    Practical yacht handling.
    1. Yachts and yachting
    2. Seamanship
    I. Title
    623.88'2'2   GV813

ISBN 0–540–07191–9

Contents

Introduction

In this guide I have tried to avoid theory as far as possible and to present a work based essentially on practical ideas. That is why every chapter is illustrated by real-life events.

The book is to some extent a putting on paper of reflections I have been able to make and experience I have been able to acquire during the course of my sailing career.

In conclusion, it has not been written from the viewpoint of oceanic sailing. I have tried to achieve a book which will be valuable for all those who go to sea in cruising yachts.

A boat moored alongside is held in position by warps, each of which has its own particular name.

The **head and stern ropes** are respectively the one which goes from the bow to the furthest forward mooring point, and that which goes from the stern to the mooring point furthest aft.

The **forward and after breast ropes** run across from the bow and stern to the quay at right angles to the boat's longitudinal axis.

The **bow and stern springs** run respectively from the bows aft, and from the stern forward.

One can see that moored in this way, provided the warps are correctly adjusted to operate together in pairs (those which prevent forward movement balancing those which prevent movement astern), the boat is held against the quay and can move neither forward nor back, remaining parallel to it. This is the classic theoretical mooring, but in practice one does not always moor with six warps. This type of mooring presents no problems when alongside a quay in tideless waters, or a pontoon which rises and falls with the tide. But alongside a quay where there is rise and fall, it will be necessary to tend the warps as the water level varies. In this case one often omits the breast ropes and uses very long head and stern ropes and springs, of such a length that the boat can rise and fall alongside the quay without the need to tend the warps. If the wind is blowing off the quay, this does present one inconvenience: that the boat lies just too far off to allow the crew to get ashore or aboard. If this happens, and one needs to have the boat alongside, it is necessary to replace the breast ropes.

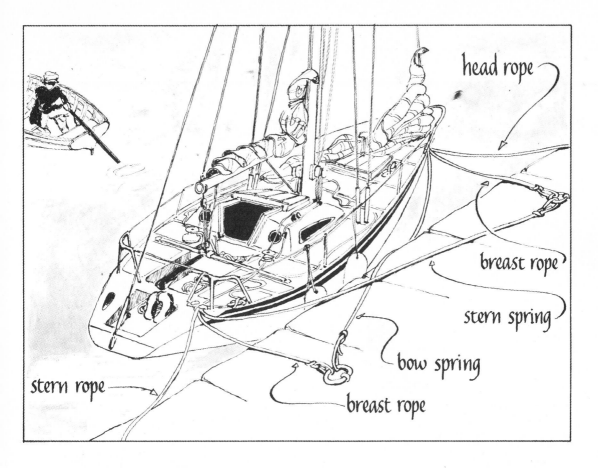

head rope

breast rope

stern spring

bow spring

breast rope

stern rope

Sometimes a shortage of mooring points on the quay may prevent the use of all these lines. In particular, if one moors to the end of a quay one will be unable to use a head rope or else a stern rope. As a general rule, for a boat to be properly moored she should have a minimum of four lines; head and stern ropes with two springs; head and stern ropes with two breast ropes; or two breast ropes and two springs. One must always moor so as to equalize the forward and backward pressures. It is no good, for example, having a spring and a breast rope astern, and a breast rope and a head rope forward. Too many people are still happy with one rope forward and one aft, made fast to whatever may be handy. Then the boat will surge forward or back according to wind and tide, and risks fouling the boat ahead or astern. There is also the danger that she will refuse to stay parallel to the quay, and the fenders, unless they are spread out from bow to stern, will no longer do their job.

If there are mooring bollards on the quay, you should make good-sized loops at the end of your warps. If the bollard is already carrying one or more warps,

11

stern rope

bow spring

then pass your loop up inside all the earlier loops before passing it over the head of the bollard. In this way the warps that were there before yours can be cast off easily, leaving yours in place. If your warp is the first on the bollard and you haven't made a long enough loop, later arrivals will not be able to arrange their lines as set out above, and you risk being unable to cast off your own when you want to.

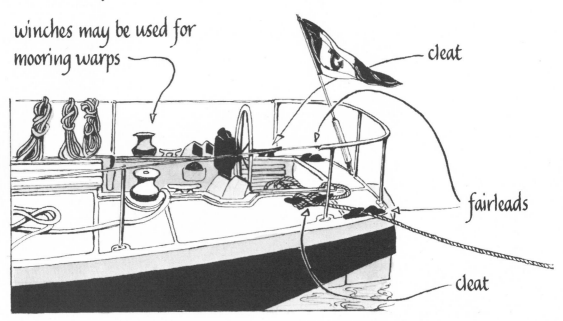

winches may be used for mooring warps

cleat

fairleads

cleat

12

Mooring alongside another boat

If a small boat comes alongside a bigger one, there is nothing to prevent the adoption of the classic system: head and stern ropes, breast ropes and springs. If the boats are of nearly equal length, one cannot use head and stern ropes. The springs and breast ropes should be carefully adjusted, so that the fenders always remain in the correct positions. Many people think that mooring like this is enough, and you sometimes see a whole series of boats alongside each other, with only the first holding all the others to the quay, the piles, or to the buoys ahead and astern. I do not regard this as good seamanship at all. The later arrivals, after mooring alongside, should put out head and stern ropes to fixed points ashore. If not, then if the wind or stream becomes strong, the warps of the first boat, meant to hold one boat but not ten, may break, and so indeed may its cleats or samson posts, which are also in danger of being torn out. In any case, even if nothing carries away it is not pleasant for the occupants of the inside boat to hear their warps, stretched near their limits, squealing in the fairleads.

Do not forget that it is for the new arrival to place his fenders, and to watch to make sure that his mooring is correctly adjusted and does not endanger his neighbour. It is always important to watch what you are doing, in order to avoid winning first prize in the competition for Idiot of the Year! We

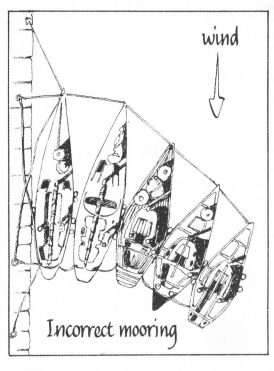

Incorrect mooring

Correct mooring

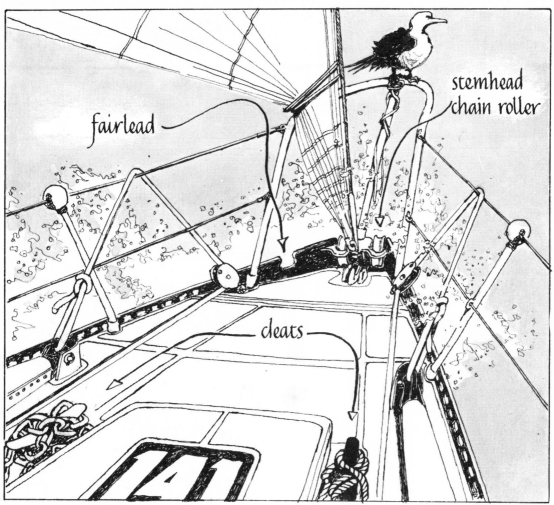

fairlead

stemhead chain roller

cleats

awarded the prize, a few seasons ago, to one of our crew who dreamed up the following stroke of brilliance: we arrived at Yarmouth with *Pen Duick VI* in the middle of the night and moored alongside a British motor cruiser. Everything went smoothly, and there was no doubt that we had managed to avoid waking the occupants of the English boat. Then one of my crew decided to slide in an extra fender. The intention was praiseworthy. To achieve it, he wedged his back against the deckhouse of the motor boat, and pushed with his feet against *Pen Duick*'s gunwale. He had not noticed that he had placed his back against a glass pane, which shattered, allowing him to fall through. The hour of the morning prevented the spectators from getting a really good laugh, even though the effect was pretty good. As for us, we didn't feel like laughing, and I called the unfortunate crew member every name under the sun. The English couple, woken up in this way, didn't feel like laughing either.

As most boats have an auxiliary motor, it is important to know how to get the best out of it. Also, yachting ports today are becoming more and more crowded, and except with a very small boat it is almost impossible to manœuvre under sail without risking an accident.

Certainly in a large vessel harbour manœuvres under sail can become extremely dangerous. It is no longer possible to save the situation after an error by fending off by hand. The arrival of thirty tons, even slowly, against a quay or another boat represents a considerable shock. With *Pen Duick III*, which had no motor, we just about managed to cope under sail, but with her 17.45 m and her 13 metric tons displacement, I think that she represented a maximum. With *Pen Duick VI* we still amuse ourselves from time to time by carrying out selected manœuvres under sail, but one must have reasonably open water and favourable conditions of wind and current. In most cases, if one wants to avoid taking enormous risks, one should manœuvre with the engine.

For success, it is essential to have a good knowledge of one's boat, and to understand certain basic principles. Far too many people are unaware of these principles, and for this reason manœuvre badly under motor without understanding why. The primary principle, most important yet very little understood, is the effect of the rotation of the propeller.

The blade of the screw which points downwards at any moment is operating at a greater depth that the one(s) above. Let us suppose a screw which, when the boat is being driven forwards, turns clockwise when viewed from the rear (i.e. is right-handed). The force **F** exercised by the water on the upper blade

18

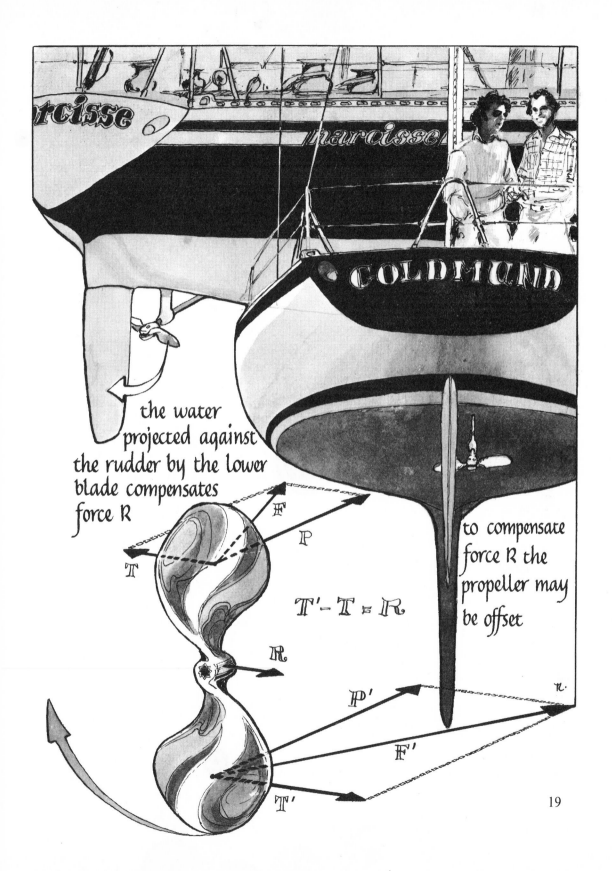

the water projected against the rudder by the lower blade compensates force R

to compensate force R the propeller may be offset

$$T' - T = R$$

19

can be divided into a thrust **P** driving the boat forward, and a component **T** at right angles to the axis of the boat. Similarly, on the lower blade the force **F′** divides into **P′** and **T′**. But, as a result of the difference in depth of water between the two blades, **F′** is greater than **F**, and thus **T′** is greater than **T**. The difference between **T′** and **T** creates a force **R**, perpendicular to the axis of the boat, which thus tends to carry the stern sideways to the right. But the propeller also projects water at the rudder, and the force of the stream produced by the lower blade will be greater than that from the upper. However, the water from the lower blade strikes against the right-hand face of the rudder, and that from the top blade against the left-hand face, if the screw is on the centreline. This effect compensates for force **R**. If the screw is not central, it is usually offset in such a way as to counteract force **R**. With the direction of rotation seen in our example, the screw would be offset to starboard. Thus while the boat is travelling forward, the effect of the rotation of the screw is negligible, and the helmsman does not notice it.

Going astern, however, things are quite different. If the screw is offset, the effect of this is added to the rotation effect. The rudder no longer receives a stream from the propeller, and now it is the upper blade which throws water towards the tuck (the underwater part of the stern), and the force exercised there is added to the rotation effect. With the motor running astern this can thus become of great importance, and with the direction of rotation chosen for our example, the stern of the boat will be driven to the left. If the boat has little or no momentum, either forward or astern, to enable the rudder to counteract this effect, the stern of the boat will move inexorably to the left.

Another effect that is too little appreciated is that of the wind on a boat manœuvring under power. With no way on, a boat will reach a position of equilibrium with respect to the wind, lying more or less across the wind direction, and will then drift sideways. Under way, the resistance to drift of the hull and keel makes itself felt, but drift is not completely prevented. It follows that when moving forward with the wind abeam, the water pressure will strike the downwind side of the forefoot obliquely, producing a tendency to luff. The same thing happens when going astern, with the water pressure bearing obliquely against the downwind side of the tuck. The rule is thus that when under way, whether forward or astern, a boat tends to turn up into the wind. Going forwards, she will not luff until the wind is dead ahead, but settles down in a position roughly corresponding to her angle when sailing fully closehauled. But going astern, she will continue to luff right into the eye of the wind, as this position is one of stable equilibrium. As the rudder is more efficient when going forwards rather than astern, if this wind effect under sternway is added to the propeller rotation or 'paddle wheel' effect, it must be allowed for to

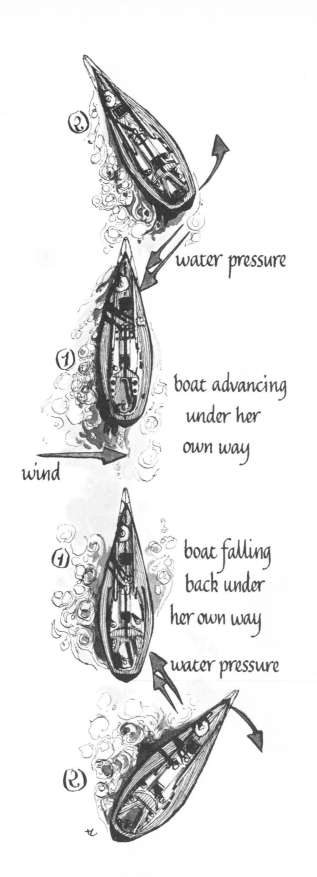

water pressure

boat advancing
under her
own way

wind

boat falling
back under
her own way

water pressure

21

the fullest extent while manœuvring. The boat will need to gather considerable sternway before the rudder will be able to counteract these effects, and before then the boat will have described a major curve, which must have been foreseen to avoid embarking on a manœuvre which cannot be completed owing to lack of space.

Beyond these general principles, it is important to have a good knowledge of the behaviour of one's boat. According to the lines of the hull, the windage and displacement, the characteristics of motor and screw, and the position of the latter, every boat has its own behaviour patterns. Clearly a boat with fine lines will gather way faster, and carry its way for longer with the motor disengaged, than one with more generous lines. In the same way a heavy displacement boat has more momentum than one of lighter displacement. A hull with a narrow fin keel will drift more when not under way than one with a long keel, but this comparison will probably be reversed under way. The boat with a short keel, and the rudder a good distance astern, will have a narrower turning circle than one with a long keel. According to the power of the engine relative to the displacement, a boat will answer her helm more or less quickly and sharply. Some propellers are designed to perform well in reverse, and one may count upon these to stop the boat rapidly. But those which fold in order to diminish their drag while sailing have very poor performance in reverse. Going forwards, the combination of centrifugal force and the reaction of the water on the blades opens the propeller easily. But in reverse, the force of the water on the blades only has to exceed the centrifugal force for the propeller to fold up. This type of propeller therefore develops very little power in reverse, and one should bear in mind that the available braking effect is thus very small. Finally, certain boats are more sensitive than others to the rotation effect of the screw, according to the degree to which it is offset and to the design of the stern. Therefore, if it is not essential to know the direction of one's screw's rotation, and recreate the little calculation laid out above to know which way the stern will tend to be thrown, it is at least vital to have discovered the answer by experimental observation.

Kicking round

If, when the boat is making no way, one places the tiller to the side necessary to turn the boat in the desired direction if she *were* under way, and then gives a short burst in forward gear, the pressure on the rudder exerted by the stream of water projected by the screw will push the stern sideways and thus turn the boat in the desired direction. This technique can change the heading by several degrees before an appreciable forward way is built up.

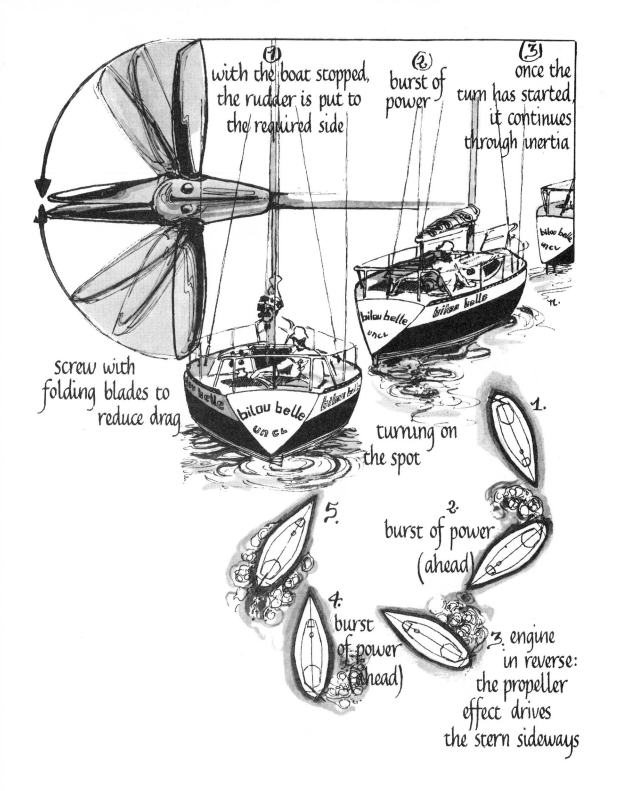

① with the boat stopped, the rudder is put to the required side

② burst of power

③ once the turn has started, it continues through inertia

screw with folding blades to reduce drag

turning on the spot

1.

5.

2. burst of power (ahead)

4. burst of power (ahead)

3. engine in reverse: the propeller effect drives the stern sideways

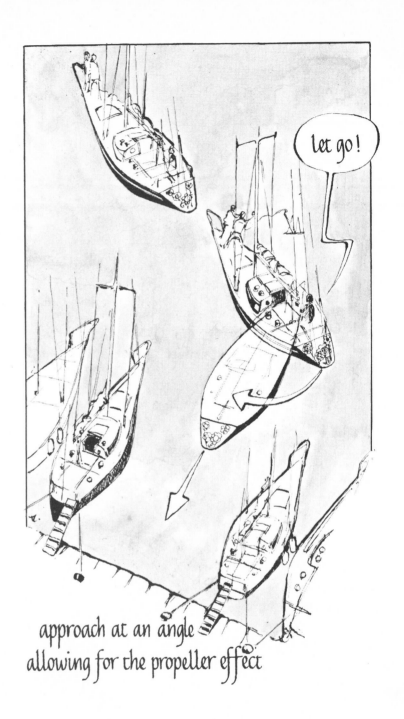

approach at an angle
allowing for the propeller effect

This effect, called kicking the stern around, can equally be used when there is a small amount of forward or sternway on. If one cuts off the power after a short burst, the turn will continue through inertia.

Turning on the spot

Using the technique of kicking round, and the propeller's transverse effect, one can make a boat turn almost in one spot. This manœuvre can only be done in one direction: that opposite the side to which the stern is thrown by the propeller effect when the engine is put astern. As far as the boat in our example is concerned, whose stern goes to port in reverse, the turn would be made to starboard.

One begins, then, by putting the wheel hard over to starboard, or the tiller to port, and engaging the engine in forward gear. The kick from the screw will drive the stern to port. Before the boat has moved more than a few metres forwards, one puts the engine in neutral, and then immediately into reverse. At the same time as the slight forward way is stopped, the propeller effect continues to drive the stern to port. There is no need to change the rudder position, as there is no intention of gaining sternway. As soon as the boat begins to move astern, one shifts into forward again for another kick, and this alternation is continued until the boat is facing in the required direction. According to the amount of room available, this manœuvre can be carried out allowing more or less forward and sternway. But if circumstances make it necessary, a boat can be turned by these means in little over her own length.

Manœuvres for coming alongside and getting under way

We will continue to study these manœuvres from the standpoint of a propeller turning in the same direction as in the preceding paragraphs (i.e. clockwise seen from astern). From what we have already seen, it is clear that coming alongside will be much easier from one side than the other, that is, coming in port side to. One comes in at an angle of twenty degrees or so to the quay. On going into reverse to stop, the propeller effect pulls the stern in, and lays the boat parallel to the quay. In this way one can easily berth in a space with other vessels close behind and ahead, or perhaps in a short inset section of a quay. If the wind is blowing strongly towards the quay, one must not get too near before going into reverse, as the wind will drive you towards the quay during the manœuvre. On the other hand, if the wind is blowing away from the quay, one must drive the bow right up to the quay before going astern, if one is to avoid finishing too far out. If there is a strong wind or current

① come in at an angle of 20° to the quay

② engine going astern: the propeller effect straightens the boat

from astern, one will need a prolonged burst of reverse to stop the boat. The propeller effect will then have longer to operate, and it will therefore be necessary to approach from a fairly wide angle. With wind or current from ahead, the opposite is true.

To come alongside starboard side to is more difficult, because in reverse the stern tends to swing out from the quay. With small craft with propellers that give good performance with the engine in reverse, the technique is to approach at a narrow angle, and at some speed. At the last moment, first with a good movement of the tiller one begins a turn to bring the boat quickly parallel with the quay, and second one gives a good burst of reverse power. Thanks to the good performance in reverse, the boat stops almost dead, while the inertia of the spin is countered by the propeller effect. If one has calculated right, the boat comes quietly alongside at exactly the expected point.

With most auxiliary yachts, one cannot behave like that. If the quay is empty behind the berth, one must come in very slowly along the quay and parallel

26

to it. Then little reverse will be needed, and the boat will stop while remaining parallel to the quay, or nearly so. With wind or current from ahead it is even easier, but things get complicated in the contrary case. Even coming in very slowly, to counteract the wind or current will involve the boat ending up at an awkward angle. The only solution is to get a warp ashore: the stern rope. It must not be tightened brutally, otherwise the stern will be pulled in and bumped heavily against the quay: just control it as needed in order to bring the boat gently to a halt. One can also send the bow spring ashore as an additional safeguard; the crew member in charge must also take care to snub the line only as needed, to avoid the bow being bumped against the quay. In this way one should be able to stop gently, parallel with the quay. The difficult case, clearly, is coming alongside in a gap. Unless the wind or current is from ahead, so that the boat will stop without needing reverse, which enables her to be eased into position by small kicks from the engine, one must resign oneself to completing the manœuvre by the use of warps. One noses the bow gently into the gap, gets the warps ashore, and uses them to bring the boat alongside.

Passing warps ashore

This is a delicate and important point. In a difficult but so far successful manœuvre, everything can be spoiled at the last moment because a clumsy crew member has failed to get his warp ashore. Equally, a slightly messed-up evolution can be saved by a warp thrown at the right moment, and successfully reaching its destination. But few people know how to throw a rope correctly; through poor preparation, it generally falls in a tangle a few metres from the boat. Many people misjudge the distance, and throwing too soon and relying on their strength, fail to achieve the impossible. If the boat is not going to get any nearer, one may try a desperate throw, but there is nothing more ridiculous to watch than warps thrown from too far when the boat is still closing with the quay, and it only needed a little patience to be within range. Instead of saving time, it wastes it, as the warp has to be recovered and re-coiled before it can be thrown again. This happened once when we were putting *Pen Duick* alongside two other boats, even though the crew had several years of experience. When that sort of thing happens I don't know where to put myself: I just pretend not to notice what is going on!

The ideal would be to have a heaving-line aboard, or preferably one ready forward and another aft. A light enough line, pulled along by a weighted monkey's fist at the end, can be thrown a long way with great accuracy, and this can save plenty of situations. The trouble is that there are already so many

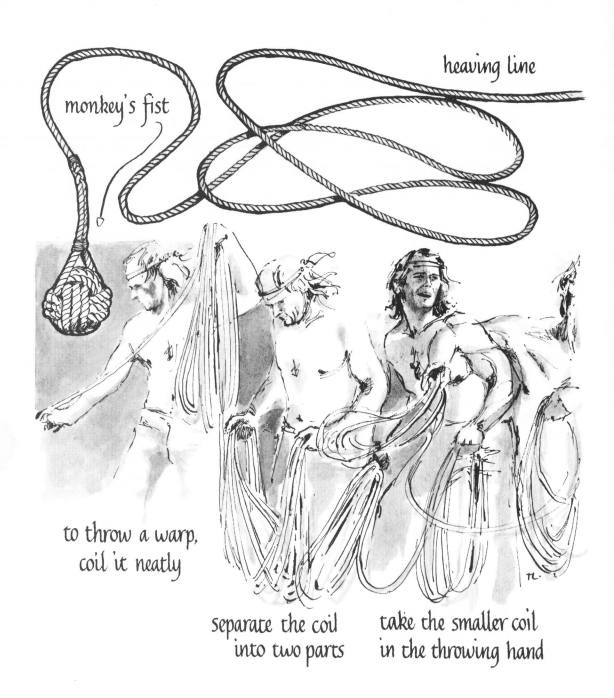

monkey's fist

heaving line

to throw a warp,
coil it neatly

separate the coil
into two parts

take the smaller coil
in the throwing hand

28

pieces of rope aboard a boat! For my own part, I admit humbly that I have only very rarely carried one, although I have often said that I always should. The most recent one was stolen from me, which proves at least that the utility of a heaving-line is recognized in certain quarters, that is unless it was the aesthetic aspect of the monkey's fist that tempted the thief.

Getting under way is usually simple enough under power. To leave under forward power, everything is cast off except the stern spring, which one must remember to have led through the quarter fairlead, and not from somewhere on the side of the boat, as often happens. If it isn't, it must be put there before starting the manœuvre. A fender is placed right aft, and then the engine is put astern. The strain on the spring will pull the stern of the boat in to the quay hard against the fender, and the bows will therefore move outwards. The engine is then put ahead, with a little rudder just to keep the stern from scraping along the quay. The angle at which you can leave the quay by this method is not very great, so the technique cannot be used if there are two or more boats alongside ahead of you, projecting well out from the quay, or if the wind is pushing you strongly against it. In this case, it is necessary to leave by going astern. To do this, the fenders are placed along the bow, everything is cast off except the bow spring, the rudder is turned to its fullest extent in the direction of the quay, and the engine is put in forward gear. One should use low revs and for a short time, as the object is to make the tension on the spring gently pull the bows in to the quay. When this point is reached, the engine is put ahead again, and now one can gently increase the power. The stream projected by the screw onto the rudder produces a thrust on it which will carry the stern out from the quay. This effect is very strong, and even with a fresh onshore breeze, one can use it to push the stern up into the wind. If need be, one can go on until the boat is at right angles to the quay. The difficulty then is in keeping the fender in position, with certain bow shapes. When, after taking account of the propeller effect, wind, current and the intended direction of departure, one judges that the boat is at the correct angle, one then moves away from the quay in reverse. If there is nobody on the quay to cast off the spring, it should have been doubled round a bollard or ring and brought back aboard before the manœuvre started.

Anchoring from the bow or stern, and mooring stern or bow to a quay

There are numerous ports where boats moor by the bow or stern to a quay, and lie to an anchor from the opposite end. It is usually stern to the quay,

① cast off
all but the bow spring

② forward power,
rudder to port

③ reverse power

fender on
the quarter

① cast off all but the stern spring

② engine going astern: the quarter
is pressed against the quay

③ forward power

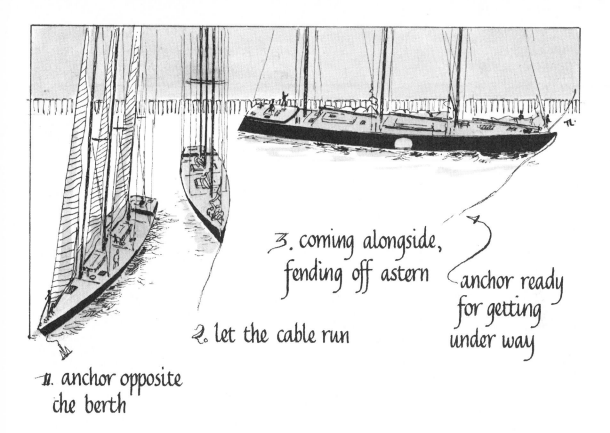

3. coming alongside, fending off astern ⟨anchor ready for getting under way

2. let the cable run

1. anchor opposite the berth

with the anchor off the bow because it is easier to rig a gangplank from the stern.

If one wishes to tuck neatly between two other boats in this manner, it is not easy. Clearly the ideal is to pass the point where the anchor is to be dropped with enough sternway to be able to steer well. One lets the chain run without checking it, and one can steer easily to bring the stern in to the chosen position. Unfortunately, one is very often obliged to anchor without way on, and then reverse into place. If you anchor thus, at right angles to the quay in front of your berth, the propeller effect will start you off in a direction so wrong that by the time you have acquired steerage way you will no longer be able to reach your berth. You must therefore anchor at an angle to the quay which makes allowance for the propeller effect on your particular boat. Wind, if there is any, must also be allowed for: the boat will not answer her helm for most of the manœuvre, so its success depends on a good estimate of this angle at the moment of dropping the anchor. That is why it is much easier to come in bows to the quay. To avoid having to shift all the anchoring gear aft, one still anchors from the bows. The upper end of the chain is attached to a warp which runs to the stern, passing under the pulpit and outside the shrouds. Travelling forward, it is easy to steer so as to bring the boat in to her berth.

Important advice

Always manœuvre as slowly as possible. There is no point in trying to impress the bystanders by charging about at full throttle: there is every danger of that ending up badly. In contrast, if one slips into neutral a little way off before coming alongside, one can lose way gradually, which leaves more time to adjust the approach. If it is necessary to alter course a little, it can be done with gentle kicks from the throttle, which is impossible if one is coming in quickly. To stop, one will not have to go full astern, which limits the propeller effect, and one will be assured of being able to stop, even though the poor performance in reverse typical of auxiliary yachts, and the considerable distance needed to stop a yacht once she is well under way, often takes people by surprise.

I am not going to talk about manœuvring with twin screws. This arrangement is very rare, and is only found on sailing boats of substantial size. In addition, manœuvring in this case is made very much simpler, and no longer poses any real problems.

Manoeuvring in port under sail

General principles

Even more than under power, manœuvring under sail requires a perfect under-standing of one's boat. In the chapter on powered manœuvres, I only touched on the concepts of turning radius and inertia, because they have only marginal importance in that field. In considering manœuvring under sail, however, their importance is absolutely fundamental, so we should begin by examining why certain boats are more or less manœuvrable, and why they have more or less inertia – that is, why with the wind ahead some carry their way farther than others.

Factors influencing the turning circle

These include the lines of the hull, but above all the design of the keel and the position and shape of the rudder.

Influence of the keel Given that it is the rudder that controls the course of the boat, and that as it is placed at the stern it is the stern which moves sideways to change the course, the boat pivots not about a central point but about a turning centre (**TC**) which describes the turning circle. This point is always towards the bows, nearer or farther according to the proportion of underwater surface near the stern, which will be opposing its sideways move-ment. Thus a boat with a long keel running right back to the counter offers great resistance to the sideways movement of the stern, and will therefore turn

34

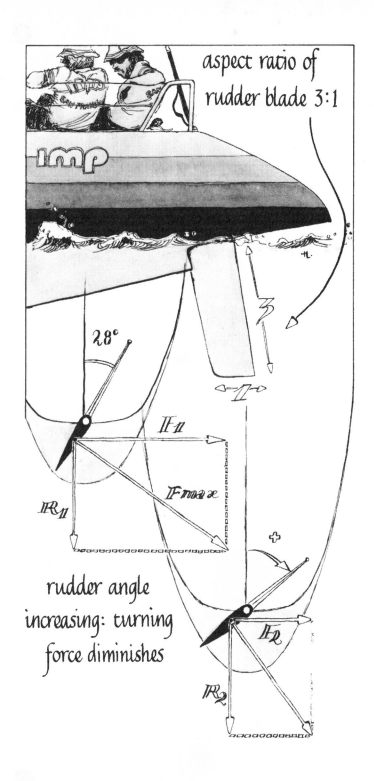

aspect ratio of
rudder blade 3:1

28°

rudder angle
increasing: turning
force diminishes

in a circle of wide radius. A boat with a narrow fin keel, on the other hand, will have a small turning circle. With this latter type of boat, manœuvres and particularly coming alongside are carried out quickly and in a minimum of space, while with the former plenty of room is needed, and there is always a risk of failure to steer.

In passing, we should note that when manœuvring one must always be aware of this sideways movement of the stern. Just because the bow has cleared an obstruction there is no guarantee that the stern will do so.

The rudder   Its effect depends upon its position, area, shape and the angle of incidence which it is given. The further aft a rudder is placed, the greater the effect it will develop, because its force is being exerted through a longer lever. A boat with a fin keel and the rudder set just behind will not have sensitive steering, while if the rudder were separated and moved further aft the boat would become more manœuvrable.

For a given area, the hydrodynamic efficiency of a rudder depends on its design. It is a surface in a moving fluid, like an aeroplane wing or a sail, and therefore it obeys the laws of fluids. For a given area and angle of incidence, the force exercised depends on the aspect ratio and the three-dimensional shape. The aspect ratio is the ratio of height to breadth, and the larger it is the greater the force developed. For a rudder placed behind the keel, there is little choice of shape. Beginning with a thickness approximately that of the keel, it will taper aft towards the trailing edge. For a suspended rudder one must choose a good profile, particularly of thickness in relation to area of the rudder, and the position of greatest thickness. Designers generally borrow a standard airfoil section.

Finally, the force developed by a rudder increases with the angle of incidence up to a certain amount, depending on the characteristics of the rudder. With an aspect ratio of 3 : 1, i.e. a height three times the breadth, which is a normal proportion for a rudder, the maximum force **Fmax** is achieved at an angle of about 28° from the fore-and-aft line. This force can be broken into components F_1, at right angles to the axis of the boat, producing the turn, and R_1 parallel with the boat's axis and producing a braking effect. If one increases the rudder angle, one can see that with the diminution of force **P**, and its angling more nearly astern, force F_2 is considerably less than F_1, although R_2 remains about the same as R_1. The boat is still slowed down, but with a much diminished turning moment. It is therefore always worth manœuvring at low rudder angles, as the turning force remains large, while the braking effect is much reduced. Even for a quick manœuvre one should never, except with a very responsive boat, slam the tiller across to 28°. The boat will be slowed down before its inertia is overcome and the turn begins. One must start with

36

10° or 15° of rudder, and then increase the angle progressively as she begins to answer.

Indeed, with suspended rudders the turning effect falls almost to zero once the angle of maximum effect is passed. The rudder loses its grip, and its effect is thus nullified. I think it is a good thing with suspended rudders to fix stops that limit the movement of the rudder, so that this position is never reached.

Turning under sail

What has been said about hulls and rudders explains why some boats are more manoeuvrable than others. But just as under power a turn can be helped by a few kicks from the throttle, or the use of the propeller effect in reverse, so

look out for the swing of the stern

the boat pivots about her turning centre

TC

under sail a turn can be assisted or counteracted, or even prevented altogether, according to the trim of the sails. If one wishes to luff, it will be done much quicker with the after sails, main and mizzen, closehauled. If one does not do this, one risks nasty surprises! Or perhaps from being closehauled in a fresh breeze you want to turn onto a run. You put the tiller up without touching the sheets. The boat begins to pay off, perhaps as far as a broad reach, heels violently, and then luffs back up again uncontrollably. If you were bearing

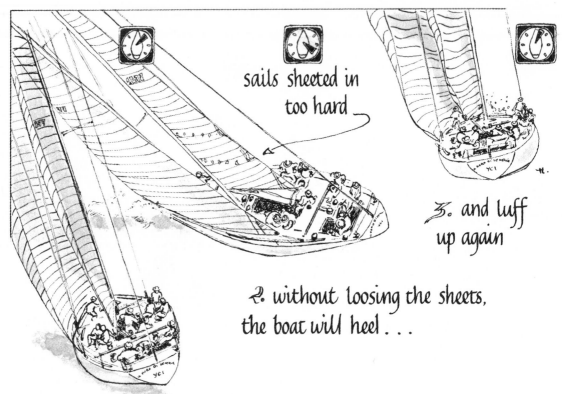

sails sheeted in
too hard

3. and luff
up again

2. without loosing the sheets,
the boat will heel . . .

1. closehauled, you want to bear away:

away to avoid an obstacle, this could result in damage. If you wish to tack in a strong wind from a broad reach, then with a light boat you must haul in your sheets, or the chop and the wind will stop you before you get head-to-wind. This results in missing stays. Manœuvring under sail, one must always bear in mind that the radius of the turning circle is much shorter when luffing than when bearing away, and in bearing away one must always be sure that the main and mizzen sheets are free to run out smoothly. If necessary, be prepared to push out the booms so that they pay out more quickly, and get these sails into proper alignment.

38

3 ... resulting in
missed stays

2. with the sails slack, the
wind and the chop will stop the boat

1. in the open sea you want to tack:

Factors influencing inertia

Hull shape is clearly one. Narrow boats like the classic 8 and 12 Metre classes will hold their way for much longer than beamy, full-bodied designs of similar size. Then there is the factor of displacement as compared with length. The light displacement boat will be stopped before the heavier one. There is also the action of the wind on the hull above the waterline and on the rigging, and also the effect of waves, which can stop a boat very quickly. Generally when manœuvring in harbour the effect of the sea is negligible. But there is still the most important effect of all, which is that of the wind in the sails. A boat under sail and head-to-wind will come to a halt very quickly, and the more so if the wind is strong. For example a slender boat of relatively heavy displacement like *Pen Duick I* has great inertia. Starting at four knots, with no sail set, she would cover at least 150 metres against a light breeze of five knots before losing way. Starting at the same speed against the same breeze, she would stop in about 50 metres with main and staysail set. And with the same sails, against a 20 knot breeze and starting at six knots, she would stop in 20 metres. Without the staysail she would go further.

A helmsman should therefore have an exact knowledge of the stopping characteristics of his boat in as many diverse circumstances as possible. To know the distances does not necessarily entail knowing them in figures. It is of no interest to know exactly whether she will cover 30 or 50 metres. What is vital is to know what those 30 or 50 metres look like, in order to be able to gauge the point where you put her up into the wind to stop in the required position. One should therefore practise training the eye. You can do this in a bay protected from sea, or under the lee of a coast, to reproduce the normal conditions in a harbour: throw a floating marker into the sea and practise coming up to it and getting there just as the boat loses all way.

In any case you will run less risk of making misjudgements if again you manœuvre at slow speed. When there is a good breeze reduce sail if your rig allows, or trim the sheets so as to diminish the thrust of the sails. This enables you to manœuvre at the desired speed, which should never be too slow, or your steering will suffer. If you do reduce sail, do so in such a way that the boat remains well balanced, and therefore responsive, because one must always remember that the manœuvre may go wrong. When you realize this, you must be able to get under way again and make a new approach. The manœuvre may fail through an error on your part, but sometimes it will be no fault of yours. An unforeseen gust may make you accelerate just at the wrong moment, or stop you too short. Harbours are surrounded by obstructions, and the wind inside is often very capricious. Try to foresee its behaviour by all means, but often this is impossible.

If you always manœuvre at about the same speeds, you will only have to carry in your head the turning circles and stopping distances for those speeds. You will therefore be more used to them, and there will be less risk of misjudgement. One can train the eye to judge speed, but nowadays many yachts carry a speedometer. If so, make use of it.

When you manœuvre, bear this in mind: if you luff up from a reach or run, the boat will begin by accelerating strongly, before the sails start to flap and she slows down. It is only when luffing from a closehauled course that she will begin to slow down right away.

Picking up a mooring buoy

The simplest case is of course where there is no stream. You need to identify the direction of the true wind. A burgee gives you the direction of the apparent wind, and from that you can estimate the true wind fairly accurately. If there

3. drop the headsail(s)

2. begin to luff

1. estimate the direction of the true wind, and of point A

4. approach head to wind, jib ready for rehoisting

are other boats in the anchorage, they will indicate the true wind direction. You adjust to your manœuvring speed and estimate the place where you will begin to luff. If you come in on a close fetch you are not likely to be far wrong about the position of point **A**, where you begin to luff so as to arrive at the buoy head-to-wind. If you arrive on a broad reach, the distance from point **A** to the final mark is far enough to be hard to assess, and often one luffs too late. If you have then gone too far past it and upwind, you will then have to come back towards the buoy with the wind no longer ahead, and your sails will not slow you nearly so effectively. Going downwind, they will always have a slight tendency to carry you forwards, even with the sheets let fly.

Generally the sail or sails in the foretriangle will have been lowered before or as soon as the boat is head-to-wind. But the jib, or a staysail if there is one, will be ready for immediate hoisting in case you fail to secure the buoy. If there is a stream running in the same direction as the wind, no problem: you only have to allow for a shorter stopping distance once you have rounded up.

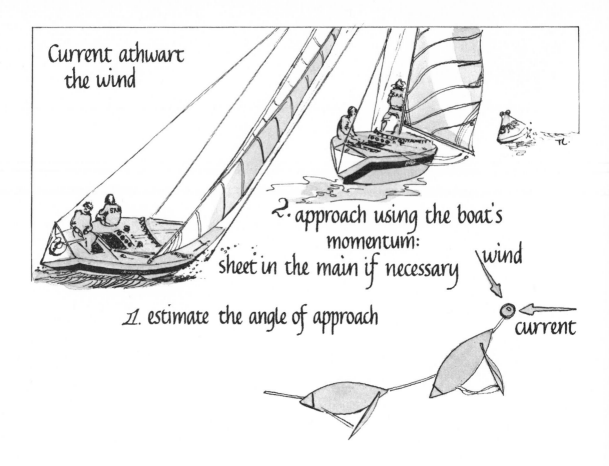

Current athwart the wind

**2. approach using the boat's momentum:
sheet in the main if necessary**

1. estimate the angle of approach

wind

current

Picking up a buoy is more difficult if the stream is across the wind. The other boats at the moorings will be lying in a direction resulting from the combined effect of the wind on their upperworks and rigging and the current on their hulls. You should therefore arrive at the buoy on a heading parallel to the others. If your boat is alone in the moorings, you have to make a guess at the angle of approach. Your mainsail let fly and flapping downwind will have less braking effect than if the boat were head-to-wind, but the stream will slow you too. So the stopping distance will be more or less the same. It is better to aim a little short, because if need be you can always add a little speed by hauling in the mainsail for a moment. On the other hand, once the buoy is picked up and well secured, the mainsail should be lowered right away: otherwise there is a danger that it will catch the wind, causing the boat to set off in circles round her mooring.

With the wind against the stream, one should approach downwind. Well in advance, the mainsail should be partially lowered leaving just enough sail area still drawing to keep the boat just making way over the ground against

Wind against current

approach downwind, mainsail partially lowered

the stream. Once the buoy is caught and the mooring warp passed, the remainder of the mainsail is lowered as quickly as possible. It can happen that as the buoy approaches one realizes that the speed over the ground is still considerable. In that case the main can be dropped completely before reaching the buoy, using the boat's way to cover the remaining distance. But the sail must be kept ready to rehoist a fraction, just in case you end up falling a metre short.

Coming alongside

It is unusual, except when you are coming alongside a boat on a mooring, to find that the wind is blowing parallel with the quay, boat or pontoon to which you want to moor. However it can happen, in which case the manœuvre is the same as for picking up a mooring buoy. Approach sailing as close to the wind as possible, at moderate speed, and finally come head-to-wind, parallel to the quay. Note that although one may pick up a buoy with the mainsail hoisted and lower it after securing, it is inadvisable to arrive alongside a quay with the mainsail up. The wind is often turbulent near quays, and there is a risk of the mainsail filling and creating problems while you are trying to moor. It is therefore better to arrive with sails lowered.

In most cases the wind will be at an angle or perpendicular to the quay. Then it becomes absolutely imperative to come alongside with sails down. It is always necessary to make a leg upwind to take way off. The jib is lowered

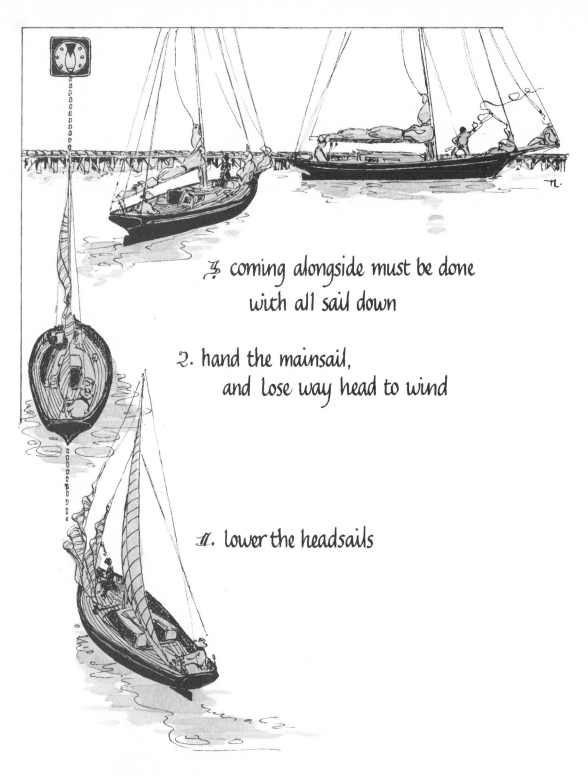

3. coming alongside must be done
   with all sail down

2. hand the mainsail,
   and lose way head to wind

1. lower the headsails

approach close, hand the mainsail
before entering the final phase—
sails down, parallel to the quay

just before luffing, and the main while head-to-wind, as that is the only way to be sure that it comes down quickly. If there are enough crew, one can of course lower main and jib together while head-to-wind. The courses will be roughly as shown in the drawings.

If the wind is blowing straight onto the quay it will not be possible to come alongside, unless there is room to run parallel to the quay for a long way, as it takes a considerable distance to stop with the wind abeam. You will have to anchor opposite your berth, and drop back to the quay by paying out chain or warp. Then all that is needed is to turn her alongside from the stern. The anchor can be left: it will be useful for getting under way, and if a little chop puts a strain on your fenders, you can bring the cable amidships and haul it taut, which will take off the pressure on the quay.

Getting under way from a quay

Offshore wind

The best thing is to leave the quay under jib or staysail. There must be a fender ready astern, because the sail forward will make the boat turn and there is

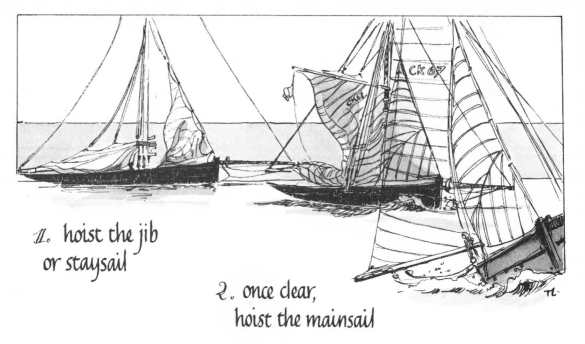

1. hoist the jib
or staysail

2. once clear,
hoist the mainsail

a risk of the quarter bumping the quay, particularly if there is a long overhang aft. Once clear, the mainsail is hoisted, assuming there is enough room. If there is not much space to leeward (the risk of collision is much greater until the boat has enough way on to luff), or if it is going to be necessary to tack soon after casting off, one must hoist the main before letting go. If the wind is aft of the beam, I don't think you are likely to find room to hoist the main before casting off. In other cases, the boom must be pushed well out very quickly, so that the mainsail does not fill. When the bow has fallen away downwind a little, the main can be gradually hauled in.

Wind parallel with the quay

If the wind is from aft, you cannot normally cast off. Even then, if the quay is clear for a long distance ahead, leaving under jib you will contrive to get away from the quay little by little. But otherwise you will have to turn the boat around with warps, and then get under way lying head-to-wind. After warping around, hoist the mainsail and cast off all but the stern spring, which must first have been passed through the after fairlead. A fender is needed where the stern will press against the quay. As the wind drives the boat backwards the spring tightens and the boat pivots about her quarter. The jib is hoisted and backed by hand or by sheeting it to windward, to help carry the bows out. When the angle to the quay and the wind is great enough, first the main

46

1. hoist the mainsail,
leave the after spring

2. the wind makes the boat fall back and
turn outwards: hoist the jib

3. the backed jib
carries the bows offshore

cast off and get under way
head to wind

wind

and then the jib are sheeted in, and the boat will gather way. One can then cast off the stern spring, which will have been doubled round the bollard on the quay if there is no-one ashore to cast off. This manœuvre works even with a slightly onshore wind, up to an angle which depends on the strength of the wind and the beam of the boat. When everything is cast off except the spring, the boat will take up a stable position at a slight angle to the quay, in the region of 10°. If the angle of the wind is more than this, one must help the

47

boat to get through the eye of the wind by pushing off with a spar or pole. On a big boat you will not be able to push her far, unless the wind is light; with a small boat you will be able to swing her out by a good few degrees even in a fresh breeze. Once she is nearly head-to-wind hoist a backed jib or foresail, which will carry her bows through the eye of the wind. Do not hoist the jib too soon, as if it does not back it will slam the bows violently back onto the quay.

Wind blowing onto the quay

In these circumstances one cannot leave the quay directly under sail. If you already have an anchor laid out outside the berth, you can haul up to it and make sail while lying to the anchor. If not, you will have to row an anchor

put down an anchor
and haul up to it

out, that is unless there is a buoy or post to which you can send a warp. If there is a quay opposite and not too far away, it might be possible to take a warp across and haul up alongside so as to get under way from this new berth.

Getting under way from an anchor

One begins by shortening in the cable, but making sure to leave enough to avoid breaking out the anchor. When the mainsail is hoisted the strain on the cable will increase, so shortening in economizes on effort later. The main is then hoisted, and the anchor broken out. Now comes the tricky moment, as one must ensure that the boat goes away on the right tack, for it is often vital to start on a particular tack to avoid obstacles or other boats. Usually the way achieved while hauling in the cable is totally checked by the process of breaking out the anchor: if it is well dug in, it will only be partially broken out by the time the momentum of the boat is lost, leaving her completely stopped.

1.
shorten in
the cable

2.
hoist the
mainsail

3.
hoist the jib aback and
pay off on the desired tack

With a ketch or schooner there is no problem. It is enough to hold the mainsail or mizzen aback on the side towards which one wants to go, and the boat will always bear away onto the opposite direction, leaving one on the required tack.

The mainsail of a sloop or cutter is not so effective, and one must pay off the bows by hoisting a headsail backed to the side opposite to the desired heading. But in this case it only needs a momentary change in the wind to stop the jib filling aback, and one will get off on the wrong tack. So great care must be taken when hoisting the headsail to make sure that it fills aback immediately.

Things become more complicated if there is a stream running across the wind. Then, when the anchor breaks out, the boat will not be properly head-to-wind. This will favour leaving on one tack, but if one has to leave on the other, it may well be impossible with a sloop. One will have to make a short

foresail

mainsail

Pen-Duick III can be steered sailing backwards, with the boom pushed to windward

Pen-Duick III: rig with two equal masts

board under mainsail. Luckily the current will be coming from the side you do not want to go and will drift you away from the danger, so the manœuvre can be carried out in relatively little room.

Casting off from a mooring buoy requires the same techniques. It is easier, because one can wait for a favourable yaw before letting go. Also, the boat is fully manœuvrable straight away, whereas after the anchor has been broken out from the bottom the chain produces drag in the water which makes evolutions more sluggish and cuts down the boat's speed. So it must be hauled aboard as quickly as possible.

Anchoring

titougn

The equipment

Every boat should carry at least two anchors, but it is no bad thing to have three. If the main anchor is lost, there is a danger that in certain circumstances the kedge may not be man enough for the job. Also, lying to two anchors to limit the swing of the boat, it is not right to have the anchor for one direction of stream weaker than that for the other, so it is preferable to carry two main ones.

As far as chain is concerned, one should have at least one with a minimum length of one shackle, that is 30 metres (16 fathoms), and a nylon anchor warp, equally of 30 metres at least. I would also recommend a second nylon cable, and two lengths of chain, each 10 metres or so in length, and heavier than the 30 metre chain.

Often racing boats do not carry the indicated minimum, all this gear being heavy and taking up stowage. Also, racing boats very seldom lie to their anchors. But for a boat making long cruises, anchoring frequently, and particularly if cruising in areas of the world where a lost anchor may be impossible to replace, the equipment listed above would hardly even suffice as a minimum.

Choice of anchors

As well as weight, which depends, as does the weight of the chain, on the size of the boat, the choice of anchors can be argued on their type.

The fisherman anchor is the oldest, and therefore has been well tried. It holds

54

well on all sorts of bottom, and in particular is the only one which will hold in thick weed. Unfortunately, on other bottoms it needs to be three or four times the weight of a modern design to provide the same holding power. If it drags, it will continue to provide a steady resistance. For the same weight, a longer, more finely built fisherman will hold better than a thicker version. I have personally used a fisherman designed for an English flying boat in the last war. Weighing barely 45 lbs, and with a shank length of almost 4 feet and arms long in proportion, it was able to dig in deeply and find firmer holding. I don't know up to what force of wind and sea it could hold a big four-engined flying boat, but for a 15 m yacht it was perfect. The only problem was that it was very unwieldy.

Anchoring with a fisherman must be done carefully, to avoid getting a turn of the chain round a fluke or the stock. This is what is called fouling the anchor.

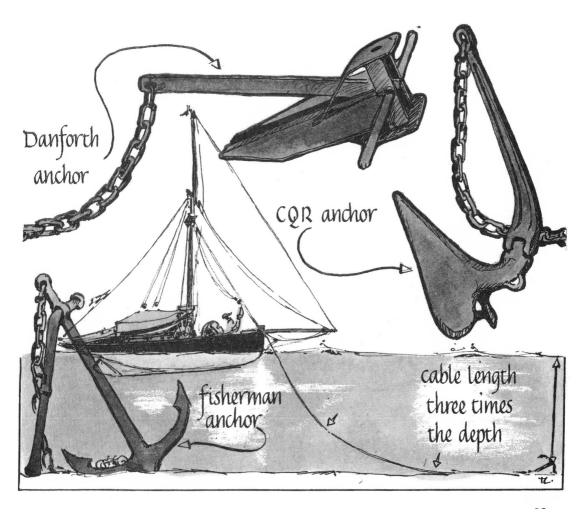

Danforth anchor

CQR anchor

fisherman anchor

cable length three times the depth

Even when anchoring has been done correctly, it can still happen later when swinging to the tide or in other conditions.

All these disadvantages – weight and unwieldiness, and the risk of fouling – tend to outweigh the advantage of better holding in weed. For this reason, the fisherman is now seldom used on yachts.

The plough anchor, of which the most widely known type is the CQR, is excellent. Like the fisherman, if it drags it goes on providing a steady resistance, in contrast to folding anchors of the Danforth type, which break out suddenly and often fail to get another hold. The only disadvantage of this type is the considerable obstacle which it presents on deck when it is stowed.

The Danforth type of folding anchor does not hold quite as well weight for weight as the CQR, but its convenience of stowage makes it very practical.

Warning: there are good and bad examples of all types of anchor. Certain badly designed fishermen never get a hold at all, and while the CQR is excellent, many imitations are bad, and the same applies to Danforth types.

Generally all these anchors and chains are made of galvanized steel. That means that within two or three years they will be covered with rust. One can have them re-galvanized, but if you want to rest easy until the end of your days, anchors and chains of stainless steel do exist. They are, of course, very much more expensive to buy in the first place.

Ground tackle

By this I mean the whole set of equipment: anchor plus chain, or anchor plus warp, or anchor plus chain plus warp. All these different parts are joined by shackles, and it is worth making sure that none of the shackles has a lower breaking strain than the chain or nylon warp. Often two shackles are needed for some joins. For instance, only a big shackle will have a wide enough opening to go over the ring of an anchor or the thimble of the warp, but its pin may be too thick for the links of the chain. It is very important that all these shackles are firmly tightened with a shackle key: if not, there is a danger that one might come undone.

Anchoring to chain only can be recommended under all conditions. It is the most secure. The chain by its weight gives the system elasticity, and if one veers a good length then even in the heaviest weather several metres of the lower end will remain lying on the bottom, protecting the shank of the anchor from being lifted, and thus preventing it from breaking out.

Anchoring to chain, one must veer at least three times the depth of water at high tide. If you can, and if the wind freshens, do not hesitate to use more. This rule applies to medium depths. In shallow water, it is not enough. For

56

example, when anchoring in 3 metres of water, if you only veer 9 metres of chain its weight will be too small to provide the necessary spring effect. Each time the boat snubs the whole chain will be lifted, and the anchor will break out.

The problem with lying to chain is the great length of chain which may have to be got up from below. On some boats this presents no problem, as it leads straight out onto the foredeck through a chain-pipe. This system is highly practical, as long as the chain-pipe is properly waterproof, which can only be achieved by means of a fitted cover or plug which can be secured. Inside the cover, one can have a hook mounted on a swivel, which enables the end of the chain to be made fast quickly. On racing boats it is usual to stow the chain low down near the middle of the boat, for reasons of weight distribution: then it is necessary to lead the chain out through the forehatch, taking care not to let it rub as it passes through and damage the hatch.

Anchoring with nylon line only is never recommended. To avoid dragging one must veer so much warp – about six times the depth of water – that the swinging area will be very large. Also there is a risk of the cable being abraded or even cut through by sharp edges on the bottom.

Personally, therefore, I prefer to use 10 metres or so of chain, of heavy gauge so that its weight is effective, and then a nylon warp. That way one does not need to bring up a long length of chain from below, while preventing the nylon being damaged by abrasion on the bottom, and the total length to be veered need be hardly longer than if using chain alone.

How to anchor

Choice of anchorage

The possibility of anchoring in harbours is becoming increasingly rare. The development of yachting has made it necessary to organize ports so as to accommodate the maximum number of boats. This has led to the prohibition of anchoring, as it requires a great deal of space because of the large swinging radius of each boat.

However, one can still anchor in some little-visited places, or in rivers and outside anchorages. By the latter I mean an anchorage in a bay which is not sheltered from all winds. If one does not know of an anchorage, one can choose one from a study of the chart. The main outside anchorages are usually shown by a small anchor symbol, but these are often intended for large ships, who are capable of anchoring in relatively great depths or putting up with an amount of sea which would make the anchorage untenable for a yacht.

Two-anchor mooring in a river

The factors in the choice of an anchorage are:

The nature of the bottom. Avoid rocky bottoms, where the anchor can jam; and weed beds, where it may drag.

Depth. Avoid as far as possible too great depth, because yachts' anchor cables are not usually very long, and most of the time the anchor has to be hauled back aboard by hand (calculate the depth of water at high and low tide from tide tables or almanac).

Current. Avoid when possible places where the stream or current is strong.

Shelter. The more closed the bay, the better the shelter from swell. One can choose a very open bay if the wind is offshore or if conditions are very fine. In any case, one must be ready to get under way quickly if the weather changes.

Arriving at an anchorage

One should come in with a minimum of sail set to remain manœuvrable but without going too fast, particularly if the anchorage is small or encumbered by hazards. Coming in with all sail set and at full speed looks brilliant if it comes off, but with the least error of judgement or mistake in manœuvring the damage will be just as spectacular.

According to the wind strength, then, one will arrive under full or reduced sail. The great rule in reducing sail is to keep a well balanced boat. A boat can remain responsive to the helm under reduced sail as long as she has way on, but if she is badly balanced and for any reason loses way she will cease to answer to the helm. For example, if after coming up into the wind to anchor the skipper decides that the place he chose will not do, he is going to have to bear away to gather speed and go out again. If the boat is only carrying sail astern, she will drift for some distance before gaining steerage way, and may even be unable to do so at all. The manœuvre will finish on the rocks, or other anchored boats, downwind. If there is only a headsail set, and the boat has to slip into a narrow entrance by making short boards, there is a risk that after going about she will bear away too far, and be unable to luff up again, even if necessary.

A sloop therefore has to arrive under jib and mainsail, and in fact will keep the sails that were in use at sea, as there will not be room to change jibs or reef just while entering the anchorage. One can keep the speed down by allowing the sails to flap to a greater or lesser degree.

A cutter can often come in under main and staysail.

A schooner, if her mainsail is large, should keep up some big headsails, but can hand all the sails between the masts. *Pen Duick III*, which had a very small main, remained very responsive under main and staysail if the wind was strong; this is normally true also for a ketch, under mizzen with jib or staysail. One must not be too under-canvassed, because then the boat will not manœuvre. If she loses way, she will be unable to regain it.

If the place is empty, you have a completely free choice of position. Where there are visible transits, it is possible to anchor at an exact spot picked out on the chart. The advantage of this is that if you have arranged for your anchor to fall exactly at the intersection of the transits, you are sure that you are in a position where you have been able to work out from the chart that you have enough water even at low tide, throughout your swinging circle. This saves you from any errors due to poor judgement of distances. But to have two transits crossing precisely at a desirable place is of course exceptional. In theory, one might anchor after taking bearings with a compass, but in practice

I do not believe in this method, unless there is a navigator aboard who has nothing else to do but look after bearings. In most cases one anchors by eye, not hesitating to take soundings. Where there is a significant tide one should note the time of anchoring so that, by using the twelfths rule, one can work out how much water will remain under the keel at low tide. The twelfths rule is the simplest way of working out depths, and for the yachtsman, who does not need to make calculations of great precision, it is the only one which he needs to know.

This rule is as follows. The sea level falls by $\frac{1}{12}$ of the range of the tide during the first hour after high water. It falls by $\frac{2}{12}$ during the second hour, $\frac{3}{12}$ during the third and fourth, $\frac{2}{12}$ during the fifth, and $\frac{1}{12}$ during the sixth. The rule is the same on the flood tide for the hours before high water.

Example. You arrive at an anchorage 3 hours 30 minutes after low water. The range of the tide on this day (in a tide table, the difference between the heights of high and low water) is 6 metres, so at low water you will have 3.75 m less than your sounder is showing, if it is well calibrated. Adding $\frac{6}{12}$ for the three hours plus half of $\frac{3}{12}$ for the 30 minutes makes 3 m plus 0.75 m : 3.75 m in all.

If the anchorage already has several occupants, you must drop anchor in a place where you will not foul the other boats. You therefore have to estimate accurately your swinging circle and those of the others. You must also bear in mind that if there is a stream, then if it is over against the wind, according to the respective strengths different boats will behave differently. Again, the swinging circles must not touch. With a strong wind over tide, sailing boats often cannot remain in a stable position. With the wind aft, they sail up over their anchors. At the end of the scope the bows are pulled back, and when broadside-on the pressure of the stream on the keel becomes greater than that of the wind on the upperworks and rigging. The stream carries a boat downstream until she reaches the end of her cable, when she is pulled round to head into it and begins to sail up again with the wind aft, and so on. The neighbours' little roundabout need not be synchronized with yours, so it is obvious that if the swinging circles touch or cross, there is going to be a nasty crunch sooner or later.

If there is no tidal stream or current, one can assume that all the boats will swing to the wind at the same time, and then the swinging circles can be allowed to overlap.

Anchoring head-to-wind

This is the most usual. One takes the way off the boat when she is head-to-wind, so as to arrive at the pre-selected anchoring site with no way left. The headsails can be lowered as soon as the boat is luffed, or immediately after letting go the anchor. Do not leave them up any longer, because they will make the boat bear away, and regain speed on a reach. The chain or warp is allowed to run out at the speed the boat falls back, without being checked, to allow enough speed for her to come up sharply. This is important, as it is the only way to tell that the anchor has got a good hold. After cable has run out to the extent of two to three times the depth, it is snubbed and made fast. It will straighten out along the bottom and then pull taut, stopping the backward drift of the boat. As she will not have been drifting head-to-wind, the bow will be pulled sharply round, so there will be a rapid pivoting movement. This sharp pull drives in the anchor. To make sure that it is holding well, it is a good idea during this operation to have a crew member put his hand on the chain outside the roller. If it holds stiffly the boat is not dragging; if the tension relaxes, and one can feel little jerks transmitted up the chain, then the anchor is not holding.

The mainsail can usefully be left up during the whole manœuvre. Its windage will help the boat to drift more quickly, and thus be brought up more sharply, and if the anchor does drag one is ready to get under way again to re-anchor.

If there is still way on when the anchoring point is reached, this does not matter seriously. Just head the boat onto the tack opposite to the one on which she will fall back: this avoids the risk of dragging the chain over the anchor. Even if it is not a fisherman, there is always a danger that the chain will catch on a point. For the same reason it is good to wait until the boat has begun to make sternway before letting go the anchor, to avoid dropping the first few metres of chain on top of it. Once the boat has brought up and the anchor is holding, enough additional cable is veered to allow for the depth at high water.

Anchoring downwind

If the breeze is light and there is no current, there will be no jerk when bringing up from head-to-wind. In these circumstances, approach downwind and let go while passing the chosen point. The cable is veered, and just before it is snubbed the tiller is put across to luff slightly. This enables the boat to be brought up sharply enough to set the anchor.

Mooring to two anchors

This can mean an open or running moor, in which the boat lies to two anchors on their own cables of more or less equal length, or other forms of anchorage where the cables are unequal, or even both anchors on one cable.

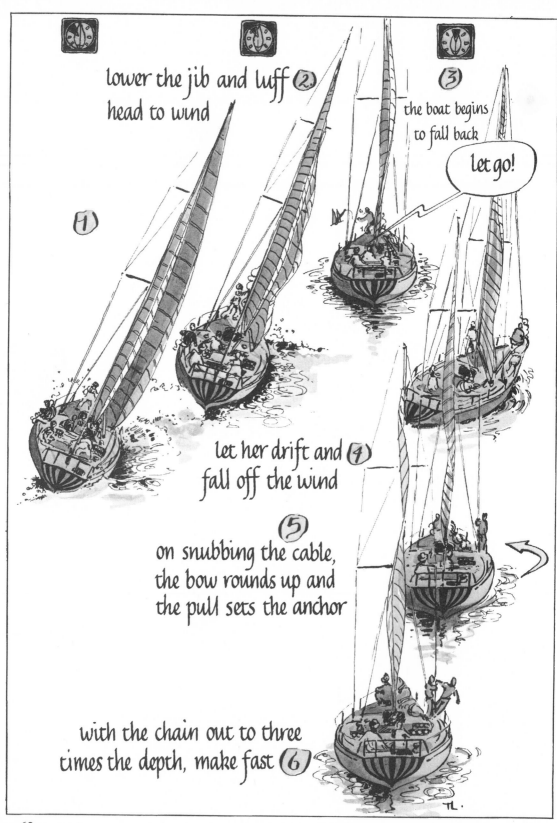

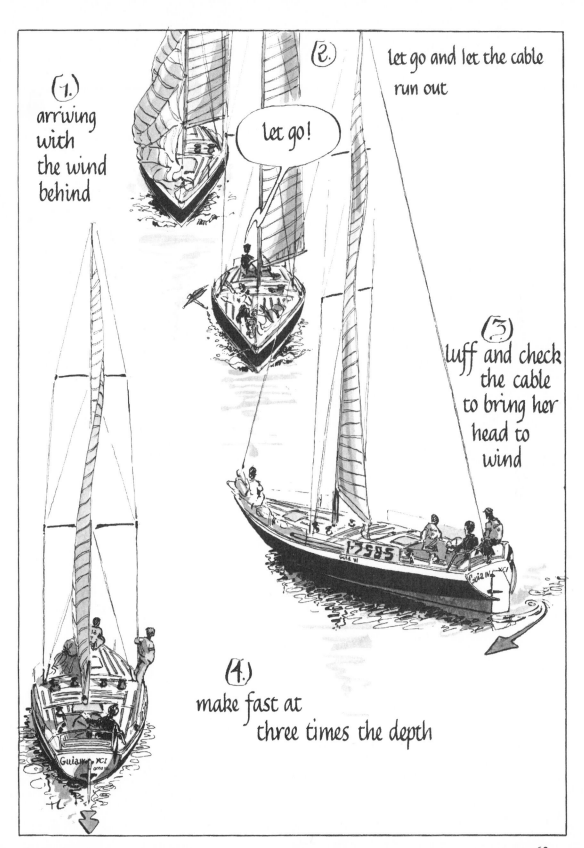

An open mooring is used if a strong wind is expected. The two anchors are laid on a line at right angles to the expected wind, in such a way that the cables make an angle of about 30° with each other. The scopes are adjusted so that there is an equal strain on each cable. The angle between the cables will limit the yawing of the boat, and so reduce the likelihood of jerks severe enough to break an anchor from its hold. One can also use an open moor to limit the swinging circle if space is restricted: in that case the angle between the cables can be whatever is needed to produce the required result.

The most usual double-anchor moor is that used in the entrance of a river, where the stream runs first in one direction and then the other. The two anchors are then dropped along the direction of the stream, so that the cables make an angle of 180° with each other. This type of mooring, which can be made running or as a fall-back moor, ensures that the boat remains in almost the same place no matter which way the stream is flowing (see page 58).

Laying the two anchors

If one has decided on a double-anchor mooring before arrival, it can be put down in the process of bringing up. The first anchor is let go over one bow, preserving enough way to carry the boat to the place where one desires to let go the second anchor, while freely veering the chain or warp of the first. One must ensure that both are well dug in by throwing a strain on first one and then the other. This can be done with the aid of the sails. If one is already anchored and wishes to lay a second anchor to reinforce the security of the mooring, then if no motor is available the second anchor must be laid from the tender. To do this, the anchor and chain are put in the dinghy. Do not try to tow the chain out: you will never make it. Lash the end of a line to the bitter end of the chain in the dinghy: it is the line that is paid out from the deck of the big boat. Once the anchor has been dropped and all the chain put over the side, you can haul in on the line and recover the chain. For a double mooring in a river, if the wind allows it is enough to drift back on the current while veering cable from the bow, and positioning the boat if need be by the means available on board. One can thus reach a position from which the second anchor can be let go. If remaining several days on such a mooring, one should untwist the anchor cables from time to time, as under the influence of the wind the boat will not always swing to the same side. As only one cable at a time is under tension, it is easy to cast off the one that is slack to undo the turns.

64

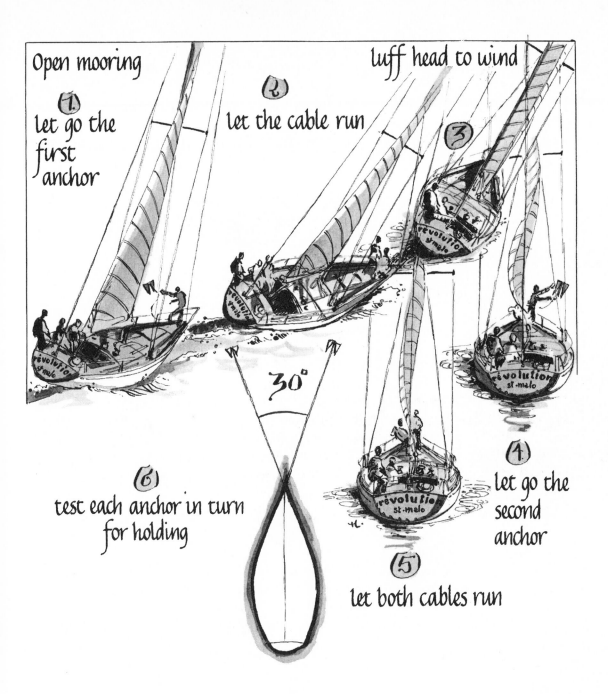

Open mooring

1. let go the first anchor

2. let the cable run

luff head to wind

3.

4. let go the second anchor

5. let both cables run

6. test each anchor in turn for holding

30°

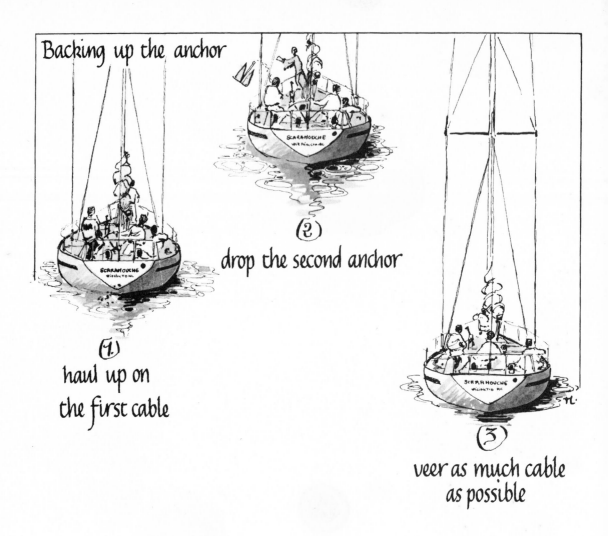

Backing up the anchor

(1) haul up on the first cable

(2) drop the second anchor

(3) veer as much cable as possible

Backing up the anchor

This is a second best method of reinforcing the mooring if it is no longer possible to lay a proper double mooring. For instance the wind may already be
too strong to permit the dinghy to be taken out to lay the second anchor.
If there is a long scope of cable out, one may begin by hauling in on the first
cable – but it is better not to, or at least to take great care, as there is a risk
of breaking out the anchor if one hauls in too far; then drop the second anchor
and veer both cables. This requires having enough sea-room astern to permit
the veering of enough cable for the second anchor, and having enough chain
or warp to provide the additional length needed on the first.

Dropping an anchor underfoot

If one cannot even back up the anchor, one can always drop a second anchor underfoot. One merely lowers the second anchor vertically from the stemhead. This second anchor does not do much good, but to some extent it will limit the yawing of the boat, and reduce the snubbing at the main cable, and thus improve its chances of holding.

Dropping an anchor underfoot

Tandem anchors

This is the strongest method. One secures on the same cable two anchors, one behind the other, joined by a few metres of chain. Disadvantages are that it is not easy to lay, and even harder to recover. When one gets to the first, and it may have to be got over the pulpit or lifelines to be brought inboard, there is still the whole weight of the chain and second anchor hanging over the side. If these are heavy, as they will be in the case of a biggish boat, one will not be able to get the anchors in by hand, and it will be necessary to make use of a halyard to lift them.

Anchors in tandem

Recommendations

Do not forget that you will not be a very popular neighbour if, after anchoring wrongly, you foul other boats who were there before you. If you realize immediately that you have left too little room, it is best to get under way again at once. However, if all that is needed is to shift your anchor by a few metres, in that case you can drop a light kedge from the dinghy in the required spot. Break out the first anchor, haul up on the kedge, and when it too is broken out re-anchor with the bower. It is far better to get this done at once, rather than having to carry out the manoeuvre, perhaps in the middle of the night, after having woken up the neighbours.

To insure against the loss of an anchor, a buoyed line may be attached to the crown. The precaution should always be taken if one anchors on a rocky bottom, or in a place where heavy wreckage or debris is likely to be found. If the anchor fouls, it can usually be recovered by the tripping line.

In an offshore anchorage, if the wind is from seaward do not hesitate to get under way at the first sign that the weather is deteriorating. Even with numerous anchors laid out in all directions in tandem, and kilometres of chain over the side, I do not think that riding out a good onshore gale in an exposed anchorage is an enviable occupation. However much confidence one may have in one's equipment, the thought of seeing something carry away, and the boat immediately being smashed to pieces in the surf which is pounding against the shore astern, is a vision horrifying enough to keep anyone awake for years. Do not forget that by the time the situation has become untenable it will usually be too late to be able to get under way, and the only course will be to sweat it out, praying that everything holds.

Arriving at an anchorage, it is important to consider the possibility that the wind will change and come from offshore. One must therefore anchor far enough from the beach to have enough sea-room to get under way in an onshore wind.

One day, in *Pen Duick III*, we dropped anchor at Ouvéa. This is one of the Loyalty Islands group, east of New Caledonia. It is an atoll, but one whose lagoon is widely exposed to the open sea except from south and east. There two long strips of land forming two islands are almost joined together. Elsewhere the edges of the vast lagoon are marked by a few islets. In the shelter of the two big islands one is well placed in a southeasterly wind, but there is no shelter from winds coming from other directions. We anchored that time in a southeaster, under the lee of the southern island which runs east to west. All along these islands on the lagoon side the beach shelves very gently. For a tender we only had an inflatable, driven by paddles, and then only very slowly, particularly against the wind. Also I anchored in the shallowest possible water, to have the shortest distance to paddle when going ashore. Well, even in this part of the world where the southeast trades blow almost all the time, you cannot be sure of anything. During the night the wind came round to the north, with enough strength to kick up a good chop, and we were woken by the thumps of the keel hitting the sand in the troughs of the little waves. There was nothing to do but get under way ... but we had no room to manoeuvre. As soon as the anchor was broken out, we would be aground, parallel to the beach. We did manage to get away, but that is another story....

Finally, before anchoring always make sure that the warp (or the end of the chain) is well secured to the boat. One feels an awful fool when the whole shooting match, anchor, chain and all, ends up on the bottom.

Equipment for anchoring and securing

From 12–13 metres upwards, every boat should have, forward:

(1) Two solid mooring cleats. Too many boats have only one, and it often creates problems because there are several warps on the same cleat. They should be large: one often needs to make fast several ropes, often thick ones, on top of each other.

(2) Two good fairleads with well-rounded surfaces, so that the warps are not chafed.

(3) At least one stemhead roller, but preferably two, which is better when anchoring with two chains.

Aft:

(1) Two good fairleads.

(2) Two strong mooring cleats, unless the cockpit winches will serve this purpose.

Is an anchor windlass necessary? Aboard a boat that always cruises with a large crew it isn't worth the obstruction it makes. With several people, an anchor can be got aboard more quickly by hand than by windlass. If occasionally the anchor is immovable, it is easy to lead the warp, or a line lashed to the chain, to a big winch. But if the boat is likely to be sailed short-handed, a small windlass is useful. The anchor will be brought up slowly, but it will come up.

tripping line

Drying
out

The use of legs

In spite of the nuisance of stowing them, it is often valuable to have legs aboard a suitable boat, and most boats are suitable. One can dry out to scrub, or to pass a low tide in a drying port. They should be rigged with one line running from the foot to the bow, and another to the stern. If the boat dries out at a forward angle, the legs must be positioned so that they will be vertical when she has dried out completely.

Clearly, legs should only be used on a more or less flat, hard bottom. It would be very dangerous to use them on a rough bottom: one of the legs might come down over a hole. Then there is a risk that the boat will fall over to that side once she has dried out enough so that the water is no longer supporting her, and the leg, at an angle instead of vertical, cannot take the weight: the leg's anchorage will be torn out, with pieces of the side and deck. Or the boat may take on a heel to this side and it may be too late to make her heel the other way. In that case, if there is still time the leg should be unshipped as quickly as possible.

Drying out alongside

To make sure that the boat leans firmly against the quay, one heels her slightly by shifting some of the weight carried aboard. Thus one might put an anchor and chain on the side-deck near the quay. Then, for safety, one takes a halyard, that of the spinnaker preferably, as it runs through a swivel block at the mast-

74

legs on a rough bottom

quickly unship the leg

and prepare for drying out

anchor and chain

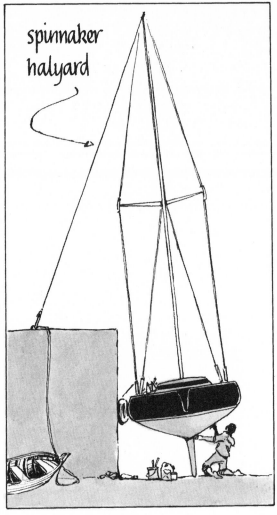

spinnaker halyard

head, and attaches it to a fixed point on the quay abeam of the mast. The halyard is kept taut as the water level falls. The disadvantage is that the line tends to make the boat pound against the quay, and if a heel has not been produced by shifting weight, she will dry rather upright.

As long as the boat dries more or less horizontally on its keel, one can replace the halyard, which needs to be tended as the tide ebbs, by a line running from a shroud to a fixed point on the quay abeam. This line slides up and down the shroud, so the boat can be left to dry out by herself without supervision. Some boats with a very narrow fin keel do not balance on it when they dry, and fall forwards or backwards. *Pen Duick III*, for example, used to fall backwards. One could dry alongside in spite of this, as long as there was a fixed point ashore, well ahead of the bows, to which a spinnaker halyard could be attached, lengthened by a warp. There was then no problem in keeping the boat upright by hauling in on the spinnaker halyard. It did not need much tension on the halyard to alter the balance of the boat as required. This was because, pulling nearly horizontally from the masthead, one had the benefit of a very long lever arm. I think that if well placed fixed points are available, one can hold any boat balanced on her keel solely by the use of halyards from the masthead: jib halyard forward, main halyard aft, and the two spinnaker halyards one at each side. With *Pen Duick III* we made things easier whenever possible by drying out, in contrast to usual practice, with the stern towards the shallower part of the bottom.

Strandings

Happily, all strandings are not catastrophic. In a great number of cases one can quickly get off again by one's own efforts. Thus, when we found ourselves aground on the beach at Ouvéa, the story of which I began in the chapter on anchorages, we were stranded lying parallel to the beach, with wind and sea forcing us on. The wind was about 20 knots, coming at about 45° over the port bow. We therefore needed to pivot the boat so as to place ourselves closehauled on the starboard tack, at right angles to the beach and heading for open water. We hoisted the mainsail, which on *Pen Duick III*, a schooner, was the aftermost sail, and hauled it in tight, which gradually headed her up towards the wind. We thus succeeded in bringing the boat head-to-wind. Then, hoisting the staysail aback, sheeted to starboard, the bows fell away to port. The staysail was then sheeted normally, and the mainsheet adjusted so that the boat remained at right angles to the beach. To make her heel, and to provide some driving force, we also hoisted the foresail and the big yankee jib, which was struck as soon as the boat was clear because it was rather too big for the weight of wind. *Pen Duick III* was the ideal boat for a manœuvre of this kind. The short keel with its ballast in a bulb, thus rounded in all directions, is ideal to permit a stranded boat to pivot. There would have been no chance of success with a long-keeled design. Also, schooner or ketch rig is particularly well adapted to making a boat pivot, and bringing her head-to-wind.

Thus, according to the boat the manœuvres for getting off will vary and be comparatively easy or more difficult, and will end in success or failure. Long-keeled boats, at least unless they have gone aground closehauled and

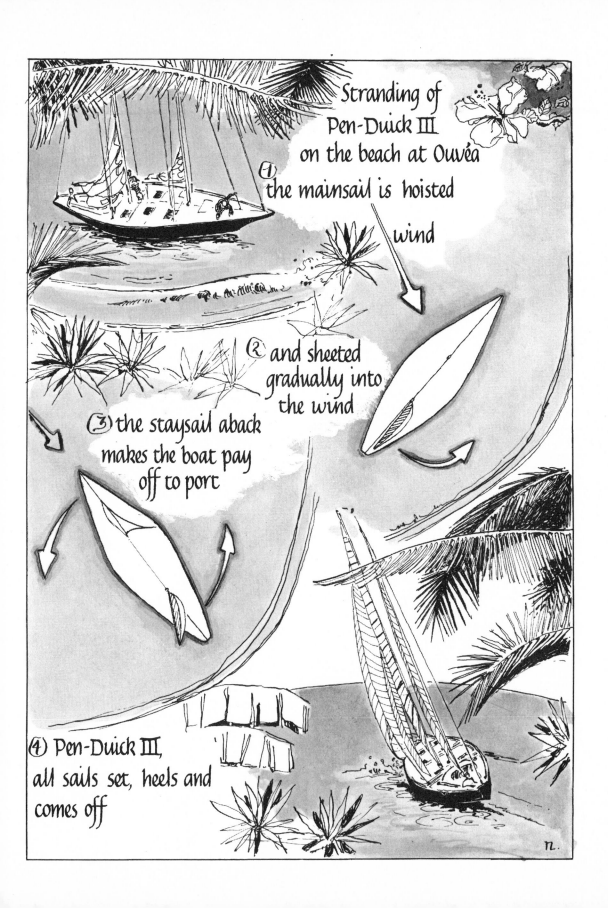

Stranding of
Pen-Duick III
on the beach at Ouvéa

① the mainsail is hoisted

wind

② and sheeted
gradually into
the wind

③ the staysail aback
makes the boat pay
off to port

④ Pen-Duick III,
all sails set, heels and
comes off

n.

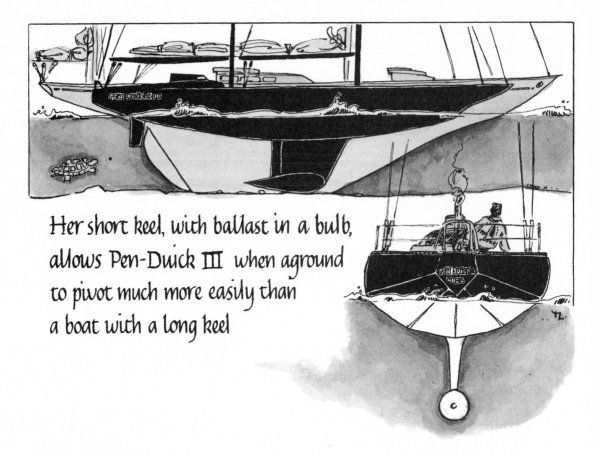

Her short keel, with ballast in a bulb, allows Pen-Duick III when aground to pivot much more easily than a boat with a long keel

on a rising tide, have no hope of getting off under sail. If under other conditions they have gone aground very gently, then no doubt they will be able to get off by using the motor: if not they will need a tow, or else the crew must row anchors out with the tender, and haul off that way.

For the other boats, with keels of average length, here are a few examples of getting off under sail. We will assume that in these situations of grounding on a beach or shoal, the water deepens in the direction from which the boat came.

The wind is directly offshore and the boat therefore went on closehauled. In this case one must lower the after sails. The jib may then be able to bring the head round as far as open water. Then the after sails are rehoisted, making sure that they do not force her to luff too soon. If necessary, do not hesitate to set a spinnaker.

The wind is obliquely offshore and the grounding was closehauled at right angles to the shore.

A short-keeled boat with two masts might possibly be turned head-to-wind,

wind

(1) lower the after sail or sails

(2) the backed jib makes her pay off

(3) all sails set, the boat sails herself off

keeping only the after sail which would be sheeted into the wind. Once through the eye of the wind, get her to bear away: the boat will now be on a course well towards open water (position **1**) with wind abeam, the best possible situation.

If one cannot get through the eye of the wind, or if the boat is a cutter or sloop, one must try to bear away, but the course for getting away from the shore will be downwind, unless one can manage to gybe. The jib will not be able to get you to bear away more than just offshore in the best conditions. To gybe, one must hold the boom right out and hoist the mainsail on the 'wrong' gybe. The turning force exerted by the mainsail may well force the stern through the eye of the wind. One can then certainly luff to achieve position **1** with a beam wind. If you have been unable to gybe, the spinnaker may perhaps drag the boat off downwind.

wind

A two-masted rig can try to pivot head to wind and then bear away to sail off on a reach

With a sloop, one must try to bear away ②, sail off downward ③ ③' or gybe ④, and luff onto a reach ⑤.

The wind is directly onshore and one runs aground downwind. It is necessary to lower the headsails and try to luff the boat with the after sails onto a close-hauled course. The jibs are then rehoisted to sail off closehauled.

The wind is diagonally onshore and the boat grounded on a broad reach. One must lower the after sails and try to gybe by rehoisting them on the 'wrong' gybe, then sail off with the wind abeam.

Aground from a broad reach, one must lower the main and try to gybe, rehoist and sail off on a reach.

Clearly the success of the operation will depend a great deal on the speed at which the boat went on, and the nature of the bottom. Muddy bottoms are very bad, because the keel buries itself deeply and resists all attempts to turn. Hard sand is the best. It stops the boat quickly without burying the keel, and the manœuvres to get off have every chance of success. Also there must be a decent wind: in light airs the boat will go aground slowly, but the sails will have no effect and she will not shift.

If one fails to get off and the tide is ebbing, it becomes necessary to ask for outside help in a hurry. This must arrive within minutes: otherwise the boat is going to be left sitting there for several hours until the tide comes up again.

If that happens, there is a risk that the side of the hull will land on stones or rock, and one must try to protect it. If one can get ashore and find some old motor tyres, that is the best: if not, one may have to sacrifice one or two sailbags. Mattresses can provide useful protection, especially for a small boat.

If the sea goes out a long way, one can take advantage of this by laying out anchors to help haul her off, taking care to dig them well in, or wedging them in a rock crevice to be sure that they hold.

If the tide is flooding, the wind is blowing onshore, and the boat refuses to pivot, or if there is no tide, it will be necessary to put out an anchor so as to haul off. One must take the strongest anchor aboard, with plenty of chain, put all that in the dinghy, and set off towing a warp lashed to the end of the chain, which will be paid out from on board. Do not try to leave carrying the anchor and towing the chain: with its weight you won't get far, and the anchor must be carried out as far as possible. If it is heavy, it will have to be balanced on the transom of the dinghy. That will be a bit grazed by the chain when it runs out, but there is nothing else to be done. Nothing remains

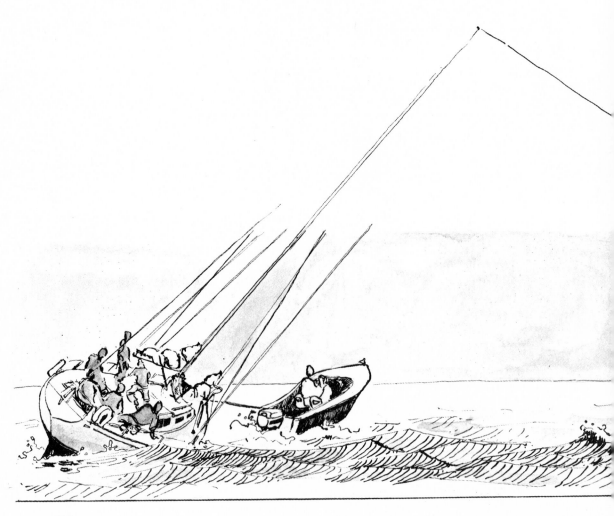

but to hope that the winches will be strong enough, and that the anchor does not drag.

If that does not work, there is still something to be tried, if the materials needed are available. A large anchor with a good length of chain is rowed out and dropped abeam, still as far out as possible. If one has an anchor weight to hold down the end of the chain, all the better. To the end that is brought back aboard the spinnaker halyard is lashed, and by hauling on this one can easily heel the boat. By doing this and continuing to haul on the after anchor, one has a chance of getting off.

One can also use the anchor to try to turn the boat head-to-sea, and then hoist sail again.

When the boat goes aground well heeled and at a good speed, at high water

or in tideless waters, one will not be able to get off with the resources on board. A powerful tug will be needed. The tow should be led to a very solid point: the foot of the mast is often best. A boat without much power can sometimes get you off by hauling on the masthead by the spinnaker halyard, to which a really long warp has been attached. The ideal is to have two motor boats, one hauling on the boat and the other on the masthead.

Use of sailbags
to protect the boat

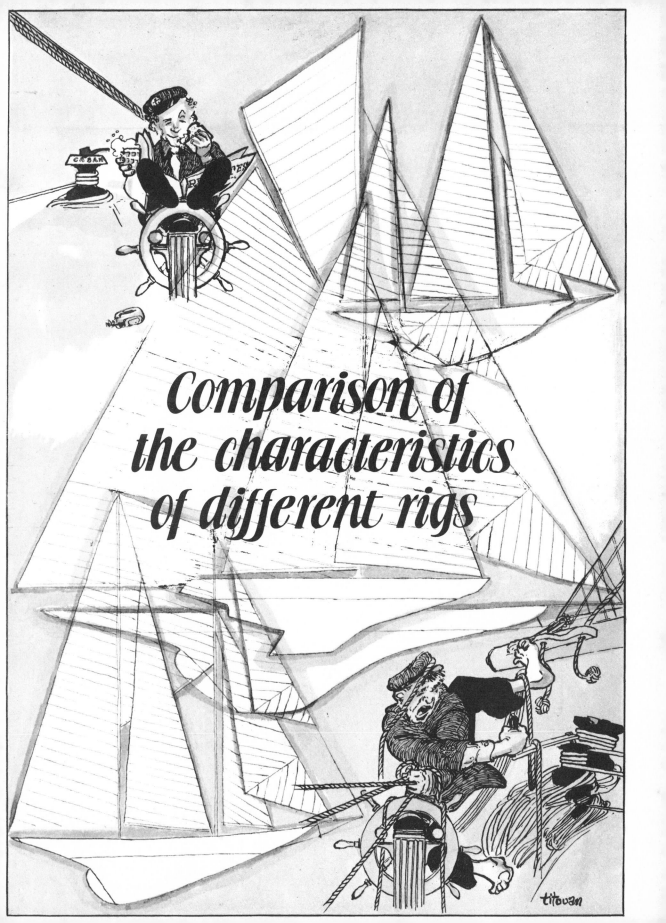

Comparison of the characteristics of different rigs

Above a certain size, which one can put in the region of 13 metres (42 feet) length overall, a cruising boat may be better off rigged as a ketch or schooner, in order to make manœuvring more simple. Not yawl rigged: that is a hybrid form of rig which I do not much like. It has the disadvantages of a ketch, without the advantages of a sloop or a cutter.

Under 13 metres, it is difficult to get a successful two-masted rig because of lack of space. One can't turn round without bumping into something: mast, shroud or whatever. The whole deck is cluttered. There is no problem on these boats, luckily, about the sails being manageable, because they are still of small area. But at this size one should do without the advantages of the schooner or ketch rig, as the disadvantages outweigh them.

On a large boat, manœuvring will be made much easier by the division of the sail area brought about by a two-masted rig. Some people think that the presence of an extra sail complicates matters. However, it is no great problem to have one more sheet to look after. On the other hand, when it comes to changing headsails in bad weather one is grateful to have smaller sails to handle. In the same way, a small mainsail will be easier to hand or reef, and there is the alternative of being able to strike the foresail or mizzen. When the wind freshens one can save a lot of headsail changes that way. It is much easier to hand or rehoist one of these sails than to change a headsail. Aboard *Pen Duick VI*, a ketch, shortening sail was carried out in the following order: no. 2 yankee, no. 3 yankee, one reef in the mainsail, two reefs, main handed, no. 1 jib, no. 2 jib, and a reef in the mizzen. While changing from the no. 3

90

yankee to the no. 1 jib, we would also change from genoa staysail to small staysail. The after sail on a two-masted rig does in fact constitute an efficient aerial rudder, and by sheeting it in less or more one can balance the boat better so that she is easy on the helm. This is particularly valuable when steering with an automatic pilot.

Certain ketches have to lower their mizzens when the breeze freshens, or they begin to carry too much weather helm. On *Pen Duick VI* one must keep it hoisted, as otherwise the boat becomes flabby when closehauled. Without the mizzen, at every wave the bow tends to slide downwind, producing a very poor windward course. The mizzen is vital for the balance of the boat.

Finally, when manœuvring in harbour, anchoring or getting off after going aground, the evolutions are done much more easily in a ketch or schooner. With these rigs one can sail backwards, admittedly only straight downwind: this manœuvre is impossible in a sloop. Without this ability to go backwards we would not have been able to get under way in *Pen Duick III* from the Chambre des Glénans anchorage the way we did. It would have needed several manœuvres with anchors. This is a small anchorage and the area in which a boat of *Pen Duick*'s draft can manœuvre is not great; and we had two boats anchored astern of us. We hoisted the mainsail (*Pen Duick III* was a schooner, so the aftermost sail was the main), broke out the anchor, and then by pushing the main boom into the wind we were able to steer straight backwards, passing between the two boats. Two-masted rigs also allow one to manœuvre in port under reduced sail, while remaining perfectly responsive, well balanced, and with small sails which are easy to get down quickly when the moment comes.

These rigs do not only have advantages, of course. The rigging is more expensive: more metres of mast, more shrouds. They are less efficient close-hauled. The after sail is working in deflected and turbulent air, and the extra amount of mast and shroud causes more wind resistance. This disadvantage when closehauled is partly counterbalanced by the ability to carry staysails when off the wind.

Is it necessary or not to divide the foretriangle between jib and staysail? Personally, I very much like having a staysail: it is a useful sail for manœuvring in harbour. In the short sudden squalls which are typical of tropical waters, it is enough to lower and furl the jib. One continues at full speed under staysail, and the jib is rehoisted once the squall has passed. While changing headsails the staysail keeps pulling and the boat therefore loses little speed during sail changes. Naturally there are some disadvantages. Unless it is boomed, it makes another sail to look after while tacking, and the inner stay hinders the

91

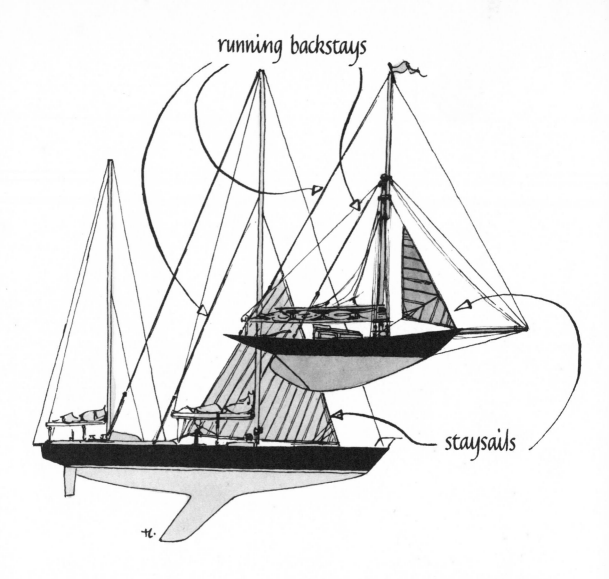

running backstays

staysails

jib in changing from one tack to the other, reducing the tacking speed and making it harder work to sheet in. There may have to be running backstays, but this in my view is more of an advantage, as with an inner forestay and backstays the mast is really well supported longitudinally. Of course one can replace the runner with a shroud attached to the mast on a level with the tang for the inner forestay, from a chainplate well aft of the mast, but I don't like this solution because if one is to be able to let the mainsail right out when running this shroud cannot be positioned correctly. It will thus be fitted too far forward to work properly. Also, to be able to use the staysail as the only headsail in strong winds, there must be runners if one is not to run the risk

92

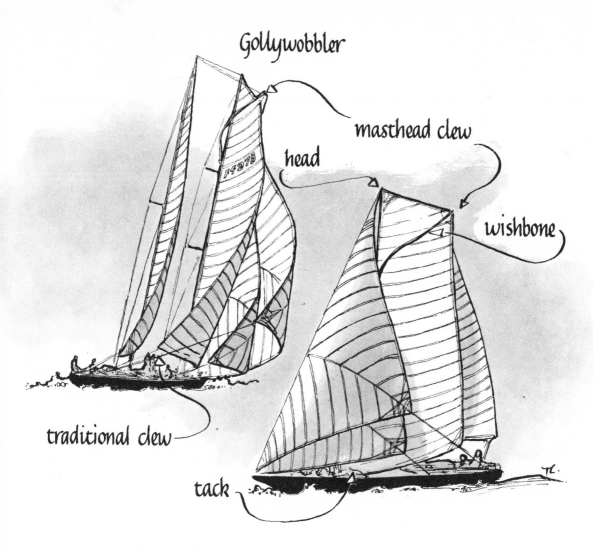

Gollywobbler

masthead clew

head

wishbone

traditional clew

tack

of being dismasted. The final disadvantage of two-headsail rigs is that they involve a few more sails to clutter up the sail locker.

To me, the ideal cruising rig is a schooner rig of the type carried by *Pen Duick III*: that is, with two equal masts. The traditional schooner rig, with the mainmast higher than the foremast, does not split up the sail plan well enough. The mainsail, providing a large sail area aft, makes some schooners carry heavy weather helm on a reach. With two masts of the same height there is a relatively small mainsail, and a foretriangle which is still of a decent size. The foresail must be cut narrow, so as to leave enough space between it and the main for the latter to perform efficiently. This rig is particularly manageable; it permits easy reductions of sail while preserving the balance of the rig, and thus also produces a responsive boat for manœuvring in port.

It performs well closehauled, and allows a large reaching foresail to be carried, which is a wonderful puller off the wind. Thanks to this rig, *Pen Duick III* could be handled with no problems by a very small crew, or even singlehanded, in spite of her 17.45 metres (57 feet) overall length.

Setting and trimming sails

This chapter is not going to deal with the trimming and tuning tricks used by racing yachts, because these often require special equipment, and constant attention from a knowledgeable crew.

Here we will talk only about basic trimming, that will allow a normally rigged cruising boat to be sailed properly and safely. Apart from performance, the yachtsman will get much more pleasure from sailing a well trimmed boat: he will have the satisfaction of having a balanced helm in his hands, instead of having to battle with a hard-mouthed or sluggish boat. Well set sails will enable him to sail close to the wind, which is much more agreeable than beating backwards and forwards getting nowhere.

First important area: the rigging of the mast. This is of paramount importance; quite apart from the driving of the boat, it can prevent your being dismasted because of wrongly adjusted rigging.

Longitudinal adjustment   The object is to achieve a very stiff headstay to enable the jib to set well. This is achieved simply by adjusting the rigging-screws (turnbuckles) on the forestay and backstays. By altering the settings of first one and then the other one will alter the longitudinal angle, that is the rake, of the mast. Generally speaking, the mast should either be vertical or raked slightly aft. It is possible that, in searching for a balanced rig, one may be obliged to experiment with mast rake. Certain boats are sensitive to this adjustment, but this is less common among modern designs. If the boat carries too much weather helm, then pulling the masthead forward will move the centre of effort in the same direction, and this may be enough to balance the boat. With lee helm, one rakes the mast aft.

96

rake of
the mast

laterally,
the mast
should be
prefectly straight

backstay
or stays

forestay, very
tight

shrouds

lower
stay

lower
shrouds

gonnagitcha   tcha   gonna

Lateral adjustment   On a seagoing boat the shrouds should be tight, and it is most important that the mast, when under load, should remain perfectly upright in the lateral sense. One can adjust the after lower shrouds in such a way that in a breeze the mast curves towards the bows, which will reduce the fullness of the mainsail and thus flatten it, but in the lateral view it must remain straight and not bend sideways. This should be checked under sail, when the boat is well heeled. Looking up the after side of the mast, the line of the mainsail track helps one to see whether the mast is bending sideways, or has an S-bend, or is perfectly straight. From this observation one can tell which shroud needs to be adjusted to straighten it.

97

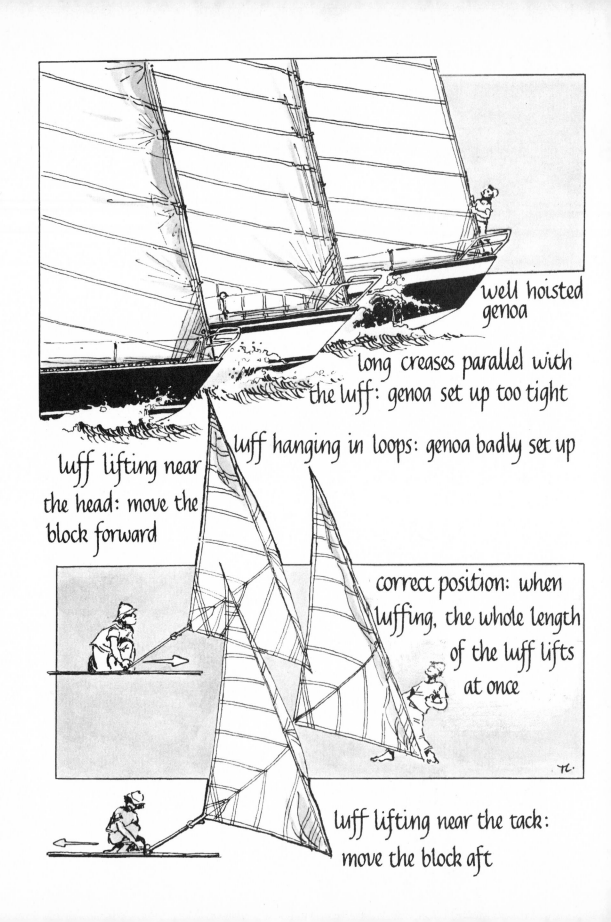

well hoisted
genoa

long creases parallel with
the luff: genoa set up too tight

luff hanging in loops: genoa badly set up

luff lifting near
the head: move the
block forward

correct position: when
luffing, the whole length
of the luff lifts
at once

luff lifting near the tack:
move the block aft

Sail setting and trimming

Headsails

First of all, the halyard should be belayed properly tight. It is incredible to see how many boats have their headsail luffs hanging in loops along the stays like bunting for Bastille Day. Aesthetically it is very ugly, and the loss of performance by the jib is considerable. It may be that your halyard winch is not powerful enough: if so, get a new one.

Where the genoa luff has a wire, this is not elastic so you set the sail up properly once and for all, and leave it at that. If the luff has a fibre rope, then the tension on the halyard must be adjusted to the strength of the wind. This has the object of keeping the maximum fullness of the sail well placed in all winds. The stronger the wind, the greater the tendency of the fullness to shift aft. Tensioning the luff-rope brings it forward. But if the wind then eases, or if the boat bears away, one must slacken the halyard. Otherwise, long creases will form in the sail near the luff-rope and parallel to it. If the wind strengthens or the boat is closehauled again, the halyard must once more be tightened.

Positioning of the sheet block must be adjusted so that the jib begins to flutter over the whole height of its luff when the bow is put up into the wind. If it begins to flap at the head, then the block should be moved forward; if at the tack, aft.

When a jib has been properly set and correctly sheeted, it is possible that the leech may still flap. In that case the leech line must be tightened until it stops flapping.

Do not carry too light a genoa for the wind: when it rises, do not delay in changing sails. Terylene or Dacron sails are very strong and do not tear except in winds far stronger than those for which the sail was designed. But they do deform, and sometimes permanently. So, apart from the undesirability of sailing with too full a sail, which heels the boat and slows her down, you run the risk of ruining your sail forever.

The mainsail

As with the jib, and for the same reasons, one adjusts the tension on the halyard to control the fullness of the sail. Here also it is essential that the halyard winch is heavy enough for the job.

The clew is attached to a traveller, whose position near the end of the boom is adjustable. In light airs and off the wind the clew outhaul should be slackened to give more fullness to the lower part of the sail. Closehauled in a good breeze it should be very tight, to flatten it.

It is important that this outhaul fitting moves easily: if not, there may be difficulty in reducing the tension along the foot of the sail, especially on a large boat, where the traveller may be hard to get at.

The mainsheet should be led to a traveller running on a thwartships track, using the whole of the available width of deck. The adjustment of this traveller is very important, because it enables the attitude of the sail to be controlled. Closehauled in light weather with some sea, the traveller should be up to windward, to allow the sheet to be let out and thus reduce the vertical tension on the sail, while still keeping the boom in close. In smooth water or with more wind, the sheet can pull more vertically.

On a sloop or cutter the mainsail can have an important effect on the balance of the boat, especially if it is big. It is for the helmsman to trim his mainsail so that the steering is well balanced. On a 12 Metre, where the mainsail is enormous, the least change of position in the mainsheet traveller can be felt at the helm.

The further one bears away, the further downwind the traveller should be moved. It is better to stop the boom lifting by means of the mainsheet than by depending on the kicking strap or boom vang.

The sail may be too full and with the fullness too far aft, even after the halyard and clew outhaul have been fully tensioned. This can indicate a badly cut sail, or deformation through long use. In this case, by bringing the traveller well up to windward one can to some extent prevent the leech from falling away, and so improve the set of the sail.

On a broad reach, when the traveller is as far downwind as it will go, one must then prevent the boom from lifting and spilling the wind by means of a boom downhaul (vang) or kicking strap. Many racing boats have a tackle or a hydraulic piston, running from the foot of the mast to a point on the boom about a third or a quarter along its length. This system, while very effective, has the disadvantage of throwing a heavy compression strain on the gooseneck. On *Pen Duick VI*, I preferred to use a semicircular track and a traveller, from which a tackle pulled directly downwards on the boom about a third along its length. This takes all the strain off the gooseneck, so much so that on *Pen Duick VI*, to prevent the spinnaker sheet from wearing itself out chafing under the main boom or against the shrouds, or even against the lee side of the mainsail, I always lead it through the end of the boom, which has the effect of exerting a strong vertical pull on it.

For a cruising boat it is not necessary to have a kicking strap permanently in position. It is enough to have a little tackle to attach under the boom and to an anchorage on the deck. It is useful for this purpose to have a continuous track on the deck with movable travellers or a series of holes, or eyebolts at

100

the deck edge, so as to be able to attach whatever one wants in the best possible position. There is nothing more annoying than those boats where you can never make anything fast where you want to. For a following wind it is very important to have a kicking strap that pulls forwards. This may be the boom downhaul tackle, which if the pull is angled correctly, can act as a boom preventer (foreguy) as well as a kicking strap.

In light airs, this prevents the boom from swinging about, and more important, in a breeze it guards against an involuntary gybe with all the risk of damage that entails. Never sail before the wind without a boom preventer (foreguy).

The mizzen is governed by the same rules as the main. Because of its position it is a veritable aerial rudder and its adjustment has a major effect on the balance of the steering.

Should one use loose-footed mains and mizzens, or not? Aerodynamically, I see no particular advantage of one system over the other. In fact, I believe that even on a racing boat one might use a loose-footed main with just as much success as one with a boom track. But aboard a boat liable to make long passages, and in particular long stretches of sailing off the wind, I do see an advantage in loose-footed sails. On a broad reach one loosens the clew outhaul so far that the foot of the sail becomes slack, and the cloth joining the luff of the sail to the footrope comes under strong tension just aft of the gooseneck (this hardly happens at all when closehauled, because the foot is stretched tight). Also, from the movements of the boat there is a continual working of this part of the sail. It ends up by wearing through, and it has happened that I have found myself with a loose-footed sail that I didn't expect!

Reaching and running sails

The spinnaker is clearly the most important. Many sailors still think that it is a sail only for racing boats. Really, they don't want to use it because they are frightened of it. These fears are quite unnecessary, and in my opinion there is no reason why a cruising yacht should not enjoy the pleasures of a spinnaker. On a run with a moderate breeze, there is a world of difference between a boat wallowing along rolling from side to side without a spinnaker and the same boat suddenly coming alive when it is hoisted, sliding joyfully through the water and completely stabilized.

Of course, aboard a racing boat with a large crew the spinnaker is kept up in strong winds, with the risks of an uncontrollable luff or broach which that involves. Cruising, one can take more trouble to look after one's equipment, and the spinnaker can always be handed without waiting for such conditions.

101

Rigging the spinnaker

aboard Pen-Duick VI

GV

1 spinnaker
2 spinnaker boom
3 boom lift
4 cord for opening boom end fitting

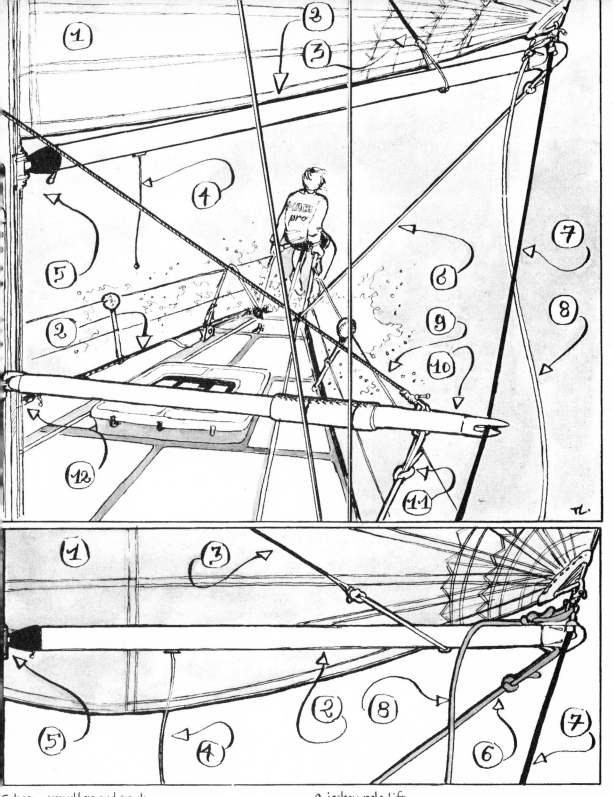

5 boom traveller and track

6 boom downhaul

7 guy: wire cable

8 sheet: rope

9 jockey pole lift

10 jockey pole

11 jockey pole downhaul

12 jockey pole and track traveller

Spinnaker rigging   Obviously this varies a lot according to the size of the boat. Thus on a large boat like *Pen Duick VI* the spinnaker pole topping lift and downhaul need their own winches, while on a small boat they would merely be made fast to a cleat, the adjustment being easily made by hand. On a large boat a wire guy and a rope sheet are needed on each side, while on a small one a rope sheet at each clew is all that is needed, as this can serve alternately as sheet and guy. On a large boat, the poles will have a mast attachment at one end and a guy fitting at the other, whereas on a small boat the ends of the pole can be identical, and when the sail is gybed the guy fitting can be used on the mast, while that on the mast moves out to take the new guy.

Whatever the arrangement a spinnaker pole should have a slider to adjust its height on the mast, a topping lift looking after the height of its outer end, and a downhaul pulling towards the bow of the boat, preventing the outer end from rising under the upward pull of the sail, and in conjunction with the guy allowing the pole to be held at the desired angle. The spinnaker guys and sheets are usually controlled by the jib winches.

Hoisting the spinnaker

The sail should have been well prepared in a spinnaker bag. It may have been carefully folded into the bag, or alternatively it may be bagged ready to be sent up in stops.

Folding a spinnaker into its bag properly must be done very methodically. I have often seen crews who were content to keep hold of the two clews and the head so that they would be left sticking out of the bag, and shovel the rest in anyhow. Doing it this way, it is even money that the sail will have a twist in it when it is hoisted. If one wishes to be absolutely sure of avoiding this, I think that the best way is:

(1) Flake down the whole length of the foot into the bottom of the bag, keeping the clews at opposite sides.

(2) Two crew each follow one leech, starting from the clew, and fold it into the side of the bag. At the same time a third packs the body of the sail into the bag, starting at the foot.

It is much better to take a little time stowing a spinnaker properly than to hoist it twisted. If the turn is near the middle it will not clear itself, and the sail will have to be lowered and the whole operation started all over again.

To stop a spinnaker, one starts at any one of the three corners. Place the two leeches, or a leech and the foot, one against the other, gather the sail into

clew

clew

foot

① pack the foot in, keeping the clews out of the bag

leech

head

② two crew members each fold one leech into a side of the bag, while a third packs away the body of the sail

105

Stopping the spinnaker

rubber bands

metal cylinder holding elastic bands

a sausage along this line, and secure it at intervals with a piece of wool yarn. This is done working from each corner to produce a sort of star, which is then put in the bag with the three points left protruding.

The material for the stops (whether wool yarn or 'rotten cotton') must not be so fragile that it snaps too soon. If it looks as if it may be, one can take two or more turns for each tie; but the ties must not be made too solid either, or they may not break at all. I have also seen stops that were put on too loosely slide until several have jammed together, when it becomes impossible to break them.

Thin rubber bands can replace wool for stops. For this a short rigid metal or plastic cylinder is needed, a few centimetres long and of sufficient diameter so that the spinnaker can pass through it lengthwise. The rubber bands are kept ready around the outside of the cylinder. The sail is passed through it and at intervals a band is flipped off the end of the cylinder and tightens onto the cloth. This is done successively from each of the three corners to produce a star-shaped furl as with woollen stops.

Generally, stopping should not be done with light spinnakers, as in light airs they will not open.

I do not find the use of stops indispensable, even on large spinnakers. By hoisting in the lee of the headsail there is no difficulty in setting the spinnaker. Of course, when changing spinnakers there is usually no headsail. In a moderate breeze one nevertheless usually manages to get it up in the end, even if it has filled too soon. If the wind is very strong when the change is to be made, one hoists a foresail: otherwise the spi will only be got up at the cost of considerable sweat, with the whole of the deck watch exhausting themselves, two by two, on the handle of the halyard winch.

The sail ready in its bag is taken onto the foredeck, where the bag should be secured with cords to prevent it from going overboard. The spinnaker pole is next put in place. On the mast it is set at the height where it ought to be when the sail is up, and so that the outboard end fitting opens upwards. The guy is put in the 'hook' of the end fitting, taking care that the line passes over the pole as otherwise it will not be able to be released when gybing. The tack of the sail is clipped to the guy, passing under the headsail and forward of the headstay. The topping lift is set up, the guy and pole downhaul tightened, the sheet is attached and secured by turns round the winch, and there is only the halyard to clip on before being ready to hoist.

If the boat is nearly on a beam reach one will set up the boom for the guy, also known as the jockey pole, before hoisting. It is easier to put it up before hoisting than afterwards.

Once the spinnaker is set, its pole and sheet are adjusted and the headsail

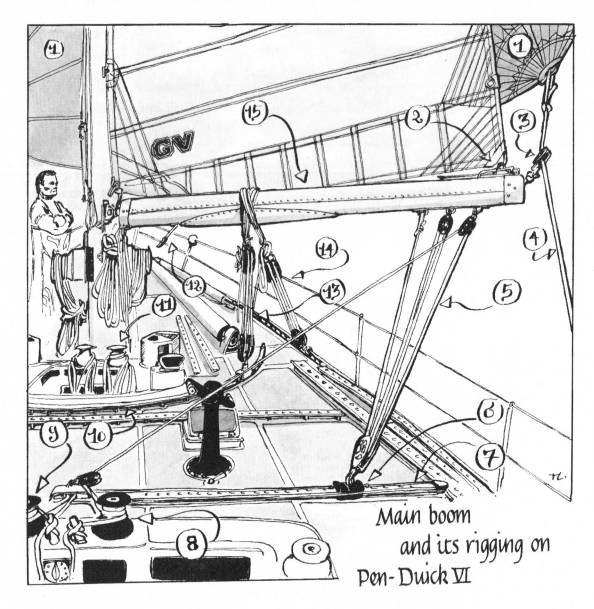

Main boom
and its rigging on
Pen-Duick VI

1 spinnaker
2 mainsail clew traveller
3 lead block
4 spi sheet
5 mainsheet
6 mainsheet traveller
7 mainsheet track
8 mainsheet winch

9 mainsheet traveller winch
10 semicircular downhaul track
11 reefing and downhaul winch
12 clew tensioning system
13 kicking strap
14 boom vang
15 loose-footed mainsail

lowered. This should be done as soon as possible, as in very light airs the spi will often refuse to fill while the headsail is interfering with its wind.

How to trim a spinnaker

(1) The pole should always be at right angles to the apparent wind. Look at the line of the burgee at the masthead, and ensure that the pole is perpendicular to that. That way, your spinnaker will offer the greatest possible area to the wind.

(2) The tack and clew should be on the same horizontal level; that is, they should be the same height above the water.

A very common mistake is to have the tack too high in light winds, as though people thought that raising it would help the sail to fill. In fact, exactly the opposite happens. If in a light wind the spinnaker is hanging sadly with its tack very high and the clew practically trailing in the water, it is often enough just to lower the boom to see it fill. The fact of stretching the foot helps to stabilize it, and also hollows the leading edge of the sail, enabling it to hold the wind.

Another common fault consists of having the tack too high on a beam or slightly broader reach. Because of the heel of the boat, the clew is likely to be fairly low on these headings, and one must therefore have a tack which is low to match.

When the spinnaker shows a tendency to collapse, it is enough to raise the pole to make it fill. Many yachtsmen, knowing this, think that that is what has to be done. If the spi collapses one must pull the sheet inboard, but above all *not* lift the pole. That way the spinnaker loses all its efficiency. It is like sailing with a completely slack jibstay: the leading edge has no hollow, because the leech closes up. It is the same with the spi.

In all circumstances, one should bear in mind that it is better to have the pole placed too low than too high. There is a serious loss of efficiency with the pole too high, but only a slight one when it is too low.

(3) The traveller on the mast should be set in such a position as to keep the pole horizontal. That way the tack will be pushed farthest outboard.

(4) The sheet should be slackened until the leading edge of the spinnaker, that is the upwind edge, on the same side as the pole, is just approaching the point where it begins to collapse.

Little problems that can occur under spinnaker

Rhythmic rolling With a strong breeze on a dead run, the boat can roll heavily. It starts with it beginning to roll a little because of the swell; this makes the spinnaker swing so that it pulls now to starboard, now to port, and thus builds up the rolling, which can become very disagreeable. One can sometimes see the main boom and the spinnaker pole plunging alternately into the water.

To control this phenomenon, the best thing is to curb the spi by pulling the clew inboard and downwards with the sheet, and correspondingly lowering the spinnaker boom. But this will probably not be enough. In that case, one must also luff a little. By coming between 15° and 20° off a dead run, rhythmic rolling will stop with most boats.

Rhythmic rolling differs with different boats, and depends on their hull

Rhythmic rolling aboard Pen-Duick VI

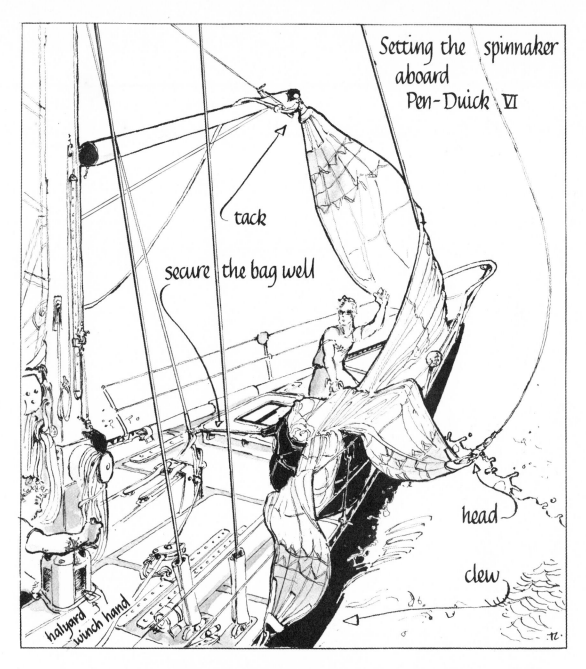

Setting the spinnaker
aboard
Pen-Duick VI

tack

secure the bag well

halyard
winch hand

head

clew

forms. For example, *Pen Duick III* did not suffer at all. One could bash along to the limit of what the gear would take, in any weather, straight as an arrow, and it was very agreeable. But *Pen Duick VI* has it badly. It is a defect which is almost universal among modern racing yachts, but if a boat is designed for cruising, it should be possible to avoid this failing.

Spinnaker wrapped round the forestay This usually occurs with a light breeze when the boat is rolling. To avoid it do not hesitate to pull the pole well down, and haul in on the sheet. Set in this way, the leeches of the sail will not be slack enough to be able to wind round the stay, and you can relax.

If the spi is already rolled round the stay the turns can be released by gybing: they will unwind by themselves. But this method will not work if the swell is in a different direction from the wind. Then it is necessary to slide the sail down along the stay by pulling on the foot by hand. If the twists have had time to get really tight, one must pull hard. Don't be afraid to tie a line to the lower part of the spi after it has been gathered together into a sausage, pass it through a block attached to the jib tack fitting, and haul it down on a winch. You will be surprised at the strength of your spinnaker, and that way you will be able to haul it gently down the stay.

Lowering the spinnaker

On a large boat such as *Pen Duick VI* one begins by passing a line round the sheet and making it fast on deck a little aft of the mast. This is necessary because the sheet is usually beyond arm's reach, and one must be sure not to let the sheet escape the grasp of the crew. On smaller boats, it is enough to take hold of the sheet by hand.

By letting out either the guy, topping lift or both, one brings the end of the pole within reach of a crew member (if the boat is being sailed with the pole fore-and-aft, one must take in on the guy while letting the topping lift out, to prevent the pole rubbing on the stay). The forward crew then opens the jaws at the pole end, releasing the tack. The spinnaker is hauled in by its sheet at the same rate as the halyard is paid out. It is up to the man on the halyard to make sure that the sail is coming aboard smoothly.

Use of the spinnaker singlehanded or short-handed

This is a method which I devised in order to be able to use the big spinnakers of *Pen Duick VI* during the 1976 Singlehanded Transatlantic Race. I didn't get much chance to use it, as I didn't have a stern wind on this race, except on one occasion. The spi was hardly up when the wind headed. I put up the jockey pole for a reach, the wind headed again, and I had to hand it. The spi was up for barely an hour, and there was no other occasion to take it out of the locker. Even so, I can report that the method works perfectly well.

The spinnaker is put lengthwise into a fabric sleeve or sheath made up to be nearly the length of the mast. For *Pen Duick VI* I designed it with a diameter

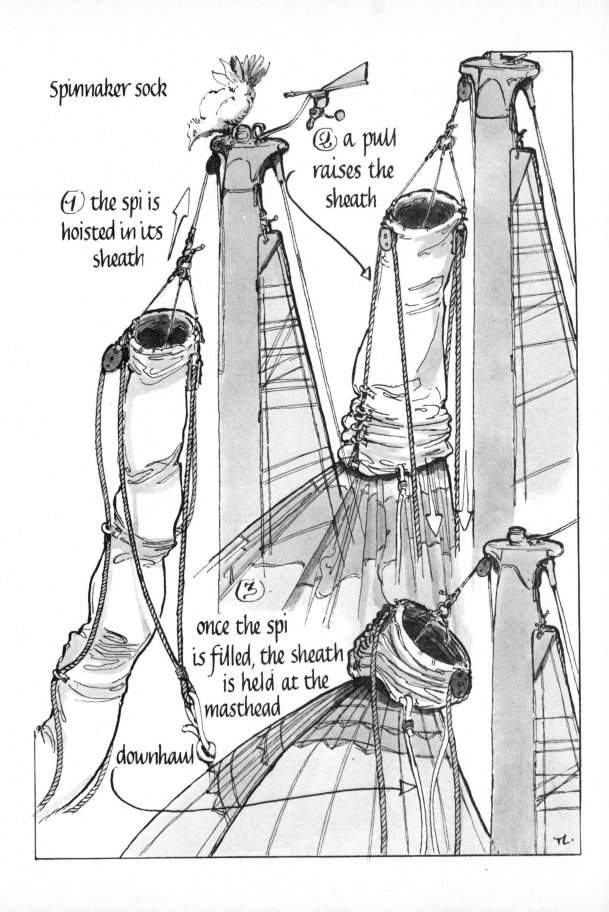

Spinnaker sock

① the spi is hoisted in its sheath

② a pull raises the sheath

③ once the spi is filled, the sheath is held at the masthead

downhaul

of 50 centimetres, so that the sail had plenty of room inside. The sheath is held in shape by aluminium hoops at each end and at intervals along its length. It narrows at the upper end to 20 centimetres across. The hoops at the ends have small rings welded on at opposite sides, at right angles to the plane of the hoop. The intermediate hoops have the same small rings, but in the same plane as their hoops.

The upper hoop is held up by two light lines running from its small rings to a strong central steel ring. From this runs a short wire strop of the same weight as the spi halyard, which is clipped to the head of the spinnaker. It is a metre long, and it is on this that the sheath remains folded up in accordion pleats when the spi is broken out.

Two small blocks are attached to the rings of the upper hoop, and through these are passed two light lines which are made fast to the rings on the bottom hoop, after being led through those of the intermediate hoops on the way. These two lines are joined into one after passing through the blocks. It is with their help that the sheath is drawn up to the head of the spinnaker. A cord, divided in two at the end, is also made fast to the rings on the bottom hoop, which is used to haul the sheath down again. The clew and tack of the sail are made fast to the small rings on the lower hoop.

To set the spinnaker one clips its halyard onto the central ring, the sail being in position forward, and it is hoisted in its sheath. The only point to watch is that the side of the sheath where the small halyard by which it is raised is located must always face aft. By day it is easy to check this, and if need be the whole cylinder can be turned round thanks to the swivel on the halyard. For night work, I painted a long stripe of fluorescent orange, such as is worn by road workers, along the after length of the sheath. One can then check that all is in order with just one flash of a light.

One then unfastens the tack from the hoop and clips it onto the end of the pole. In the same way the clew is unfastened, to be attached to its sheet. Take care while doing this that the cord which will be used to haul the sheath down is on the after side of the spinnaker.

Nothing remains but to raise the sheath. If the sheet has been belayed so that the spi begins to fill at once, the sheath will soon be lifted above the sail quicker than you can pull it up. The halyard and downhaul of the sheath are then belayed at the foot of the mast.

To hand the spi the pole is allowed to swing forward and the sheet is paid out. The sail being thus emptied of wind, pulling in on the downhaul makes the sheath come down again with no difficulty, swallowing up the spi as it descends.

The manœuvres of hoisting and recovering the spinnaker by this means

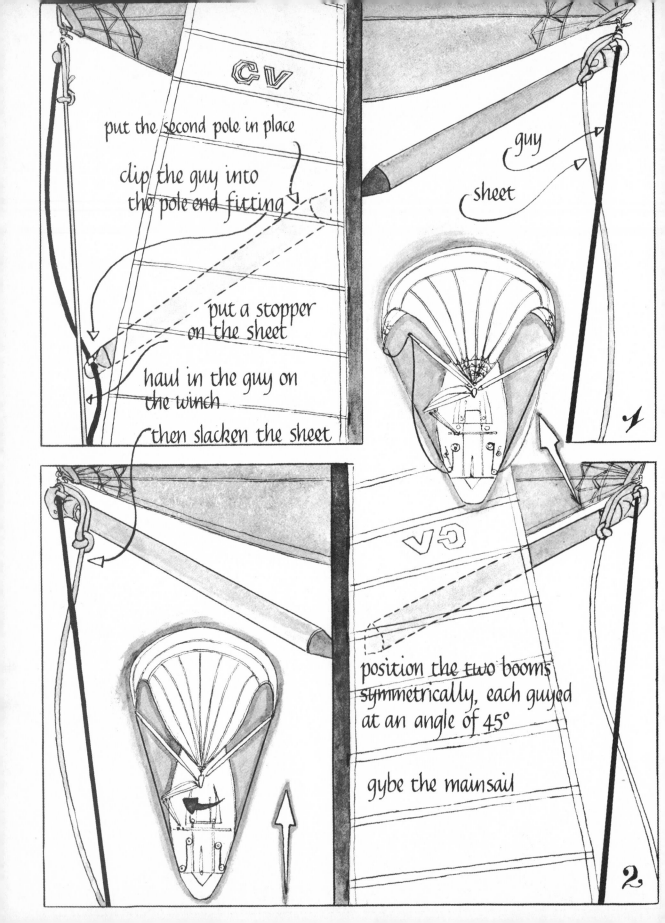

put the second pole in place

clip the guy into
the pole end fitting

put a stopper
on the sheet

haul in the guy on
the winch

then slacken the sheet

guy

sheet

position the two booms
symmetrically, each guyed
at an angle of 45°

gybe the mainsail

2.

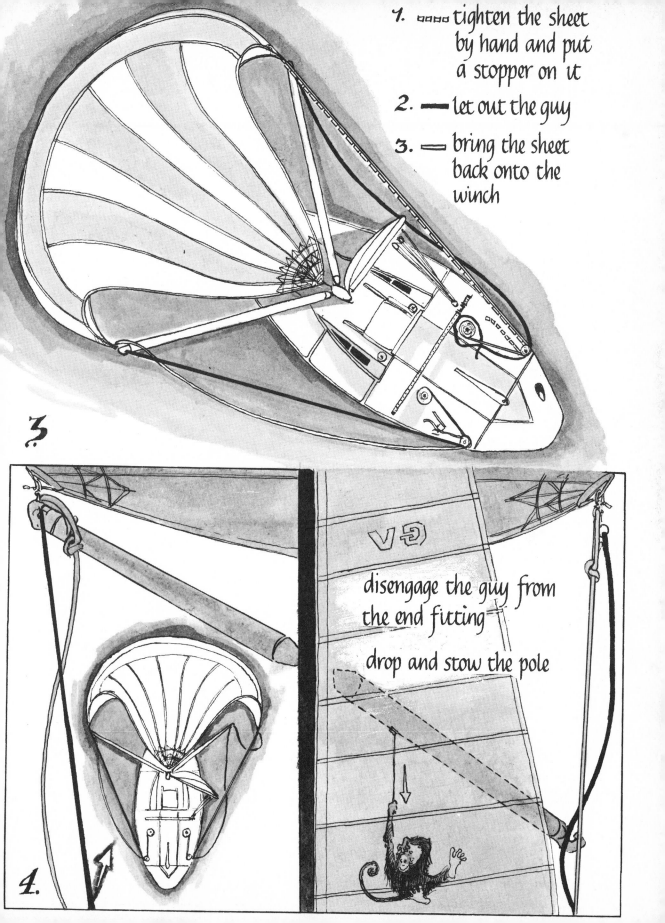

1. ▭▭▭ tighten the sheet by hand and put a stopper on it

2. ▬ let out the guy

3. ▭ bring the sheet back onto the winch

3.

disengage the guy from the end fitting

drop and stow the pole

4.

should be possible on a broad reach or a run, but not on a beam reach, as with the heeling and the windage of the sheath (on *Pen Duick* the weight and windage are by no means negligible) there would be a risk that it would get away from you and finish up flying free from the masthead.

Gybing the spinnaker

On small boats the pressure on the pole when running is never so strong that it is impossible to disengage the inner end from the mast traveller. This end of the pole is then clipped to the ring on the downwind clew of the sail, which becomes the new tack. The opposite pole fitting is detached from the other corner of the sail, which becomes the clew, and attached to the mast traveller.

One can manœuvre quite large spinnakers this way. For instance, this is what is done aboard 6 Metre boats, whose spinnakers must be something like 80 square metres (860 sq ft) in area. That is probably the maximum size for this method, as I remember that some days this could not be done by one crew member, though we were usually racing in sheltered waters so that even in strong winds there was no sea, which made things a good deal easier.

On large boats

I will not describe the method of dipping one pole, as this cannot be used on a large cruising yacht because it requires a number of crew and may involve casting off the inner forestay. Aboard *Pen Duick VI* it requires a helmsman, a man on the pole topping lift, one on the downhaul, two on each coffee-grinder (perhaps four), two tailing on the lines, two on the mainsail, one on the mizzen, and one on the foredeck to put the guy in the hook of the pole end fitting once this has been passed under the stay. This adds up to thirteen men, if there are no running backstays to look after, which is a full racing crew.

However, this method is indispensable when racing round the buoys. It is the only one which allows one to gybe round a mark without loss of time, approaching on a beam reach on one gybe and leaving on a beam reach on the other. On a cruising yacht this is a manœuvre which one is very unlikely to need, and gybing with two poles is always preferable.

One begins by setting up the second pole, fixed to the mast at the same height as the other one. The downwind guy, which is slack, is clipped into the new pole's end fitting. One takes in the topping lift, but not too much: make sure that the end of the new pole remains well below the foot of the spinnaker,

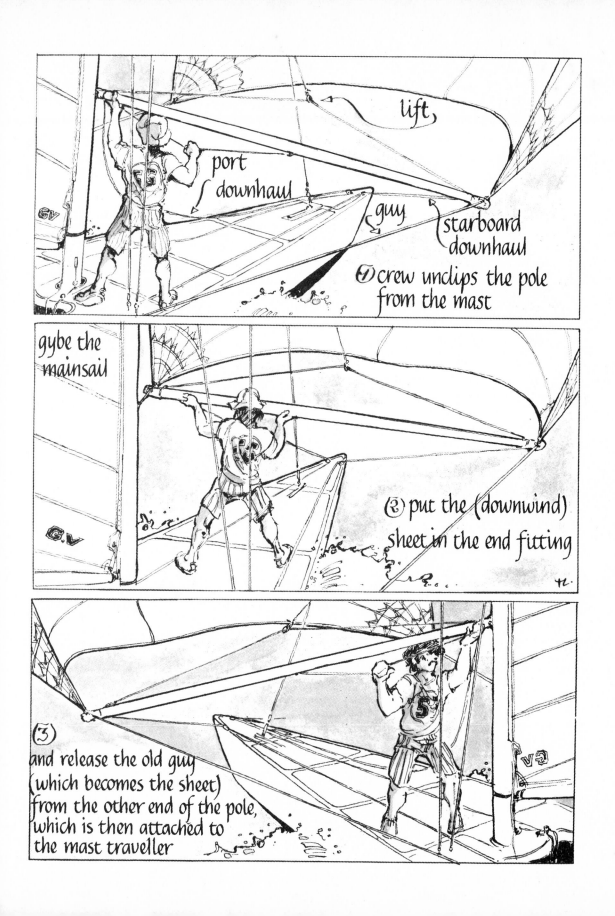

lift,

port
downhaul

guy

starboard
downhaul

① crew unclips the pole
from the mast

gybe the
mainsail

② put the (downwind)
sheet in the end fitting

③

and release the old guy
(which becomes the sheet)
from the other end of the pole,
which is then attached to
the mast traveller

to avoid the risk of tearing it. The pole is hauled upwind to an angle of about 45° to the bow. The downwind guy is hauled in, while paying the sheet out as necessary, until the end of the guy can be put in the new pole's end fitting. The downhaul should not be let out too far, so that the guying angle remains about 45°. The topping lift is adjusted. The two poles are now more or less symmetrical with reference to the bows.

One can now gybe the mainsail.

To remove the old pole, now the downwind one, the guy must be slackened. To do this, the sheet is tightened by hand as much as possible (unless there is a sheet winch) and a stopper is put on it. One can then pay out the guy, slackening the topping lift and pulling on the release cord for the pole end fitting. The guy will come free from the pole and the sheet must then be hauled in quickly. (It will have been put on the winch as soon as the guy was taken off.) One must haul the sheet in fast, because now that the spinnaker is no longer held out by the old pole, it will have insufficient support. The old pole's lift should be paid well out, without allowing the pole to fall into the water, so that the end immediately drops below the edge of the sail, removing the risk of tearing it. The end of the old pole is hauled forward and then dropped to the deck.

The jockey pole or guy boom is a small spar which is set from the side of the mast, at right angles to the fore-and-aft line of the hull, to hold out the spinnaker guy so that it does not bear on the shrouds when the pole is well forward. It also has the effect of reducing the compression strain of the guy on the pole. This spar is not indispensable, but it is so useful that one is astonished at having been able to sail without it. In fact, it only put in its first appearance a few years ago.

Other sails

The spinnaker staysail A light sail of spinnaker weight nylon whose tack is fastened to the weather edge of the foredeck, a little aft of the tack position for the jibs. It can be hoisted with either the jib or the staysail halyard. The less strong the wind the less useful this sail is, and in light airs it must be lowered as it interferes with the spinnaker and becomes an actual nuisance. When there are several, the smaller ones are hoisted as the wind slackens.

Aboard a cutter rigged cruising yacht this sail is not necessary, because its best performance is on a beam reach in a good breeze and in those conditions the genoa staysail will do almost as well.

The big boy or blooper made its appearance on racing yachts in the early 1970s. It is an amusing and very effective sail, giving a good increase in speed,

120

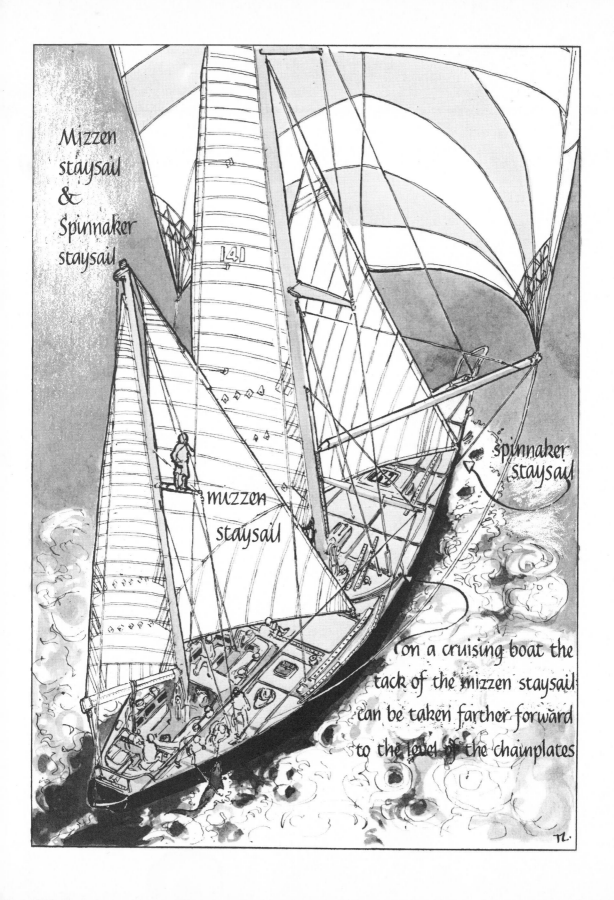

Mizzen
staysail
&
Spinnaker
staysail

141

spinnaker
staysail

mizzen
staysail

on a cruising boat the
tack of the mizzen staysail
can be taken farther forward
to the level of the chainplates

TL.

and there is no reason why it should not be used on a cruising yacht. A large and very light nylon headsail, it is cut by the sailmaker to a special design which differentiates it from a ghoster. Its tack attaches to the bow, and it is set outside and downwind of the spinnaker. It is not hoisted right to the mast-head, to avoid tangling with the spi.

To hoist this sail I think one must have a second spinnaker halyard. I would not advise using a jib halyard as the sail will pull too much to the side, pulling the halyard off its sheave and jamming it. The big boy is sheeted to a block near the stern and used with the wind astern or on the quarter. It has to be handed when, coming more onto a reach, the spi begins to press too heavily on it. One can then hoist a spinnaker staysail, as it will begin to become effective on this point of sailing.

Mizzen staysail on ketches   This sail is very easy to set and strike and is most effective, especially when the wind is a few degrees abaft the beam. On racing boats mizzen staysails are not always of maximum size, owing to rating considerations. But aboard a cruising yacht you have no need to deprive yourself, and you can have a large one which will be tacked on the chainplate for the weather mainmast shroud. It can cover the whole mizzen, and if it has been cut with a high enough clew can be sheeted through a block on the end of the mizzen boom.

The luff-wire of the staysail often comes in contact with the backstay, and the cloth covering the wire usually becomes worn very quickly at this spot. Sailmakers put on leather reinforcement, but that does not usually last very much longer. I have found the best solution is to sew on a length of thick plastic tubing, slit open down one side so that it can fit straddled over the wire and lie on both sides of the luff of the sail.

A special form of this sail is the **mizzen spinnaker**. It is quite a small spinnaker which presents no handling difficulties, and has the advantage over the mizzen staysail that it does not block the view to leeward, as its foot is cut much higher. It also has a bigger area, and on a broad reach it pulls much better.

Aboard *Pen Duick VI* the mizzen staysail is used with the wind forward of the beam, round to about 10° aft of it. Further aft than that, the mizzen spinnaker is set. On a very broad reach or a run the mizzen has to be handed to keep the mizzen spi pulling. Running in light airs, the only way to keep going is to use light sails of large area pulling well, while handing the mainsail and mizzen. We therefore carry the spinnaker, big boy and mizzen spinnaker. This combination pulls well.

On racing boats, again because of rating penalties, one cannot have as big a mizzen spinnaker as one would wish. In particular, according to the sail plan of the boat, it is sometimes necessary to cut it rather narrow. That is

122

Spinnaker, big boy
and mizzen spinnaker

mizzen spinnaker

spinnaker

F5999

F5999

big boy

040

tack of big boy

big
boy

the sheet of the
mizzen spi
passes through
a block at the
end of the
boom

big boy
sheet

tack of the mizzen spi secured by
two lines, one attached to the weather mizzen shroud,
the other to a cleat at the foot of the mainmast

TL.

the case on *Pen Duick VI*, where our mizzen spi is a bit narrow across the shoulders. But for cruising these problems do not arise, and one can have a pretty little spinnaker.

At the tack, the mizzen spi has two lines: one leading forward, which can be made fast to a cleat on the mainmast, for example, and the other running aft. Aboard *Pen Duick VI* this latter is led as high as possible on the mizzen shroud or lower stay, or the running backstay. By playing with these two lines one can adjust the position of the tack of the sail. The sheet is led via the end of the mizzen boom, and by adjusting the sheets and halyard one can let the spinnaker out to leeward, so that it does not take the mainsail's wind. In practice it becomes an extension of the mainsail.

With the wind nearly abeam, one must not hang on to this sail for too long in a freshening breeze, as under those conditions it will produce in the boat an uncontrollable tendency to luff.

The big foresail on schooners   Schooners have always carried between their masts a big four-sided reaching sail that occupies the whole available area, and partly overlaps the mainsail. Americans, who have a lot of schooners, call this sail a gollywobbler; it is also called a fisherman's staysail. Being very large, it makes a considerable difference on a reach. On *Pen Duick III* it was even carried closehauled in light winds with good results.

The luff of the sail uses the normal mast track on the foremast, so there is no problem in setting or striking it. On *Pen Duick III*, to improve the sail's efficiency on a run or broad reach, I used to set it with a wishbone spar, which required several crew, but without the wishbone one man could handle the sail without difficulty.

Trim is adjusted by playing with the tension of the halyard as for a mainsail, and with the two sheets: the lower one which acts like a foresail sheet, and the upper one which runs to the head of the mainmast.

Reducing sail

When the wind freshens and a boat exceeds a certain angle of heel, sail must be reduced because she is slowed down. A boat too heavily heeled has such misshapen underwater lines that her passage through the water becomes difficult, and this has a considerable slowing effect. One can easily lose a knot for a few degrees of excessive heel. In addition life aboard becomes most uncomfortable; and finally, by hanging on to sails that are too big in wind forces that they were not designed for, you run the risk of deforming them.

These are the real reasons for shortening sail, not the fear of seeing the mast go over the side. A boat designed for the open sea, meant to withstand whatever

124

the weather may throw at her, should be rigged so that she can be knocked down flat without anything carrying away. One can always be taken by surprise by a violent squall and have the boat overcanvassed for the time it takes to shorten sail. One must have confidence in the rig, because if not one spends the whole time worrying, and that spoils all the pleasure of sailing.

Some boats go better when heeled than others. Thus a 12 Metre, with an exceptionally fine-lined hull, reaches its best speed at a large angle of heel. *Pen Duick VI*, a boat of average beam and with easy balanced lines, hits her best form with a relatively high heeling angle, in the region of 30°. *Pen Duick III*, beamier and with a wide, shallow hull section, goes badly when heeled and should never be allowed to go over more than 25°. Sail is shortened by reefing the main and mizzen, and using smaller and smaller jibs.

Reefing the mainsail and mizzen

When **roller-reefing** the boom is rotated using either a lever and ratchet system or a worm gear and crank, so that the sail is wound down around the boom. The disadvantage of this simple system is that it is difficult to keep a good sail shape beyond a certain number of rolls. In practice, even if the designer has had the forethought to provide a hollow near the gooseneck to take the luff of the sail, this will quickly be filled up, and after that the luff will make a thicker roll and therefore roll up more quickly than the rest of the sail. Also, as the sail rolls up, the leech should be pulled aft. The sail being triangular, the leech comes obliquely to the boom and therefore tends to wind in towards the mast as it is rolled down, transforming the sail into a veritable sack. Only on small boats is it possible to pull the leech aft sufficiently, and so more and more the preference is for slab-reefing.

With a well designed **slab-reefing** system the sail can be reefed as quickly as by rolling, and a good sail shape is always maintained. For this method the boom should have a strong hook at the gooseneck on each side. A little aft of the place where the leech cringle will come down to the boom, there must be a belaying point on one side of the boom and a sheave on the other. The reefing line will then run up from the belaying point through the leech cringle and back down through the sheave to a winch, which can be fixed either on the boom itself or on deck. On *Pen Duick VI*, after the sheave the line re-enters the inside of the boom, runs to a vertical sheave near the gooseneck, and from there goes via a block at the foot of the mast to a winch in front of a cockpit which is situated a little aft of the mast.

Generally the reefing lines are not left in place on the sail. There is no serious disadvantage in having them permanently in place, but personally I prefer to

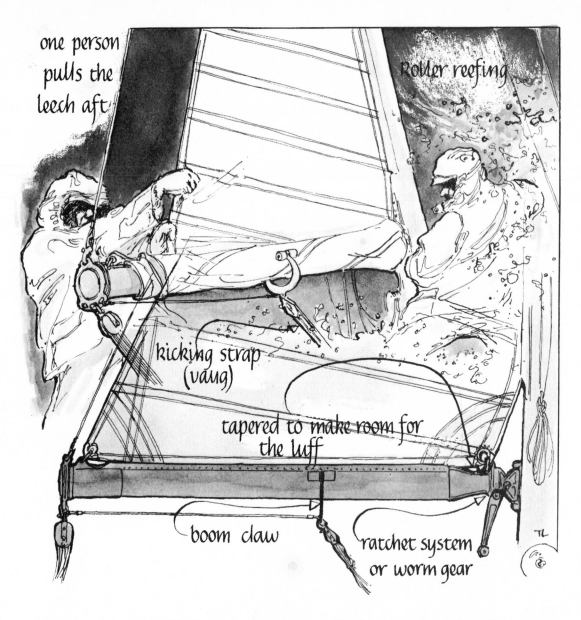

one person
pulls the
leech aft

Roller reefing

kicking strap
(vaug)

tapered to make room for
the luff

boom claw

ratchet system
or worm gear

remove and replace them on each occasion. To have cordage frapping permanently against the leech risks causing a certain amount of chafe.

On a large boat like *Pen Duick VI*, the reefing operation starts by climbing onto the boom to pass the line through the reef cringle. Equally, one can wait until the halyard has been slacked off enough to bring the cringle within arm's reach of the deck, but in a strong breeze the sail flogs violently, and in view of its size on this boat it becomes quite a battle to get the line through the cringle. On a smaller boat this can be done with no difficulty.

Once the reefing line is belayed to its fixing point, the halyard is slacked off while beginning to haul in the line at the same rate as the sail comes down. When the luff reefing cringle reaches the level of the boom it is placed on one of the hooks on the gooseneck. It is often necessary to release one or two of the sail slides above the cringle from the mast track. The reefing line is made fast and the halyard set up and belayed. The sheet is hauled in, and nothing is left except to thread a lacing through the eyelets, or tie the reef points. But the sail is pulling normally already: the lacing is merely to secure the bunt of the reef.

To shake out the reef it is enough to cast off the lacing or points, slacken the halyard so as to be able to take the luff cringle off its hook, and hoist the sail, letting out the reefing line as needed and replacing the slides that were freed from the mast track.

Is a topping lift useful in these manœuvres? My view is no, if there are several people in the crew. On *Pen Duick* I never rigged a topping lift except when singlehanding, when I had one on the main boom. Then, when slackening the halyard there was nobody to haul in the reefing line or sheet to position the boom over the required place on the deck. It would therefore land after bouncing across everything, and then bang back and forth among the winches and cleats as the boat moved. The topping lift prevented this carnage. But with a crew I can see no use for it, and as there is no point in having a rope without a purpose I have abolished it.

Changing headsails

On modern racing yachts headfoils are in use with single, or more and more frequently double, luff grooves. They give the headsail a better aerodynamic performance than hanks, and the double-grooved foils also permit a replacement headsail to be hoisted in the other groove before the first is lowered, so that the boat is never without a headsail. I advise against these systems on cruising boats, as they can be more trouble than they are worth. The jibs are difficult to hoist and lower. The cloth can chafe in the groove and tear. The luff wires can pull out of the groove at the bottom and jam. The use of hanks is safer, and should be used on a cruising boat where high performance is not the first priority. I also, and very strongly, advise against double forestays. Happily they have almost totally disappeared, after having been fashionable for twenty years. With this system one cannot have a properly stiff support for the sail; the hanks on one stay always manage to hook themselves onto the other hanks or stay; and if the spinnaker gets wrapped around two stays one cannot get it down.

127

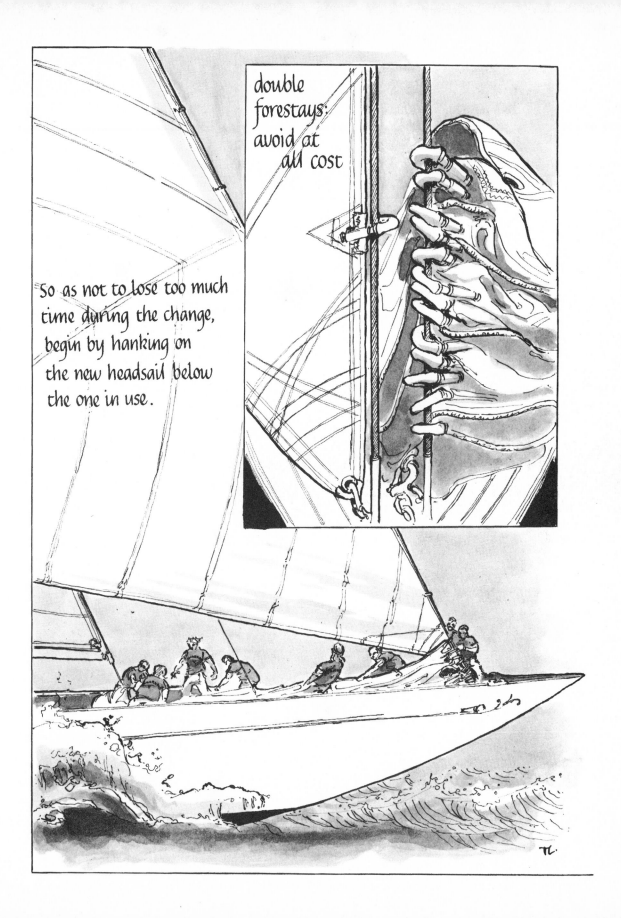

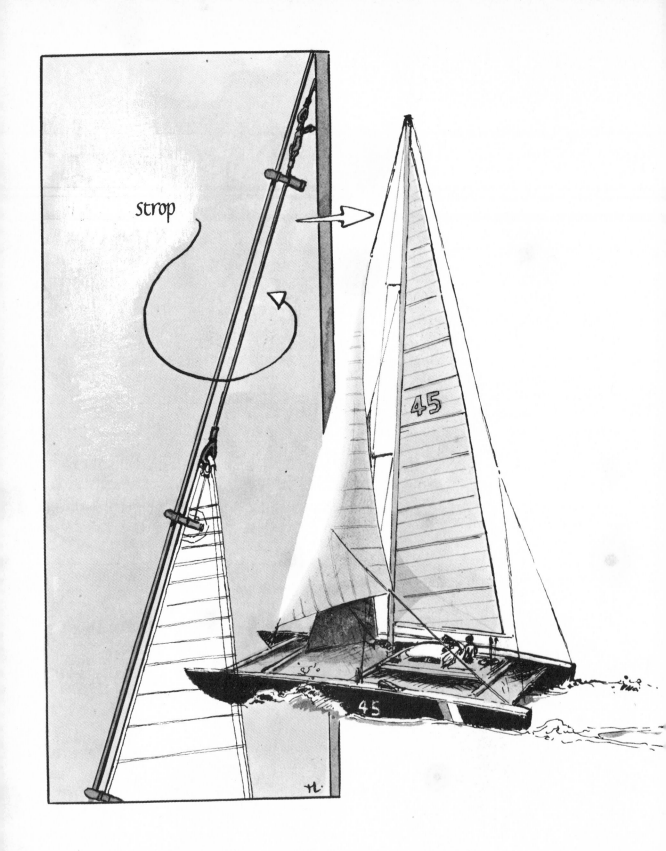

strop

If the need to shorten sail is not urgent, then to avoid wasting time one begins by hanking on the new headsail underneath the one in use. The old sail is then lowered and unhanked while a crew member changes the sheets and adjusts the position of the sheet blocks. The old headsail is stowed and the new one hoisted. If everything goes smoothly the boat should not be without a headsail for long.

For small jibs that do not reach the masthead, your sailmaker will no doubt supply wire strops to join the head of the sail to the halyard, so that even with their shorter luffs it is still the wire part of the halyard that turns around the winch drum. If he doesn't, ask him to, as the rope part of the halyard is not designed for taking the full tension.

On a large boat, to lower a headsail in a breeze the helmsman can sometimes help the foredeck crew by luffing. He must not do this too early, as he will risk having lost all way before the sail is down and will then be forced to bear away: the situation will then be difficult. He must wait till the jib has come down a fair way before luffing. On a large boat with a short-handed crew, or even singlehanded, it is still perfectly easy to lower a large headsail and prevent it from falling in the water.

Take great care, when a headsail is being hoisted or lowered, that no part of it is allowed to slide overboard between two stanchions. That can happen very easily when the bow pitches downwards, and one must watch out to prevent a small bit of canvas from slipping cunningly over the side. For if too much goes over (and once a small bit is in the water, it will quickly pull over a lot), it will form a great bag in the water which you will not be able to recover by hand, and which will buckle or tear off your stanchions. As a safety measure, one can make a sort of net by threading cord from the deck to the lifelines, which will prevent this type of accident.

A genoa on a boat the size of *Pen Duick VI* is difficult for one man alone to recover, once it has fallen in the water. During the Singlehanded Transatlantic Race I used a simple and effective technique. I hoisted two Y-shaped lines on the downwind side of the genoa with the spinnaker halyard. The outer ends were made fast to the stemhead and the foot of the mast, and the other two at intermediate positions on the lee rail near the middle of the foredeck. If you haven't got lazy-jacks of this kind already made up, they can easily be improvised from any old bits of rope. The genoa slides down inside this sort of net, and lands safely on the foredeck.

To avoid getting a headsail halyard twisted round the stay requires a little method. When a headsail is lowered, as soon as the foredeck hand has the head of the sail in his hand he releases the halyard and secures it to the pulpit or stanchion, on the weather or lee side as he prefers, but never allowing it

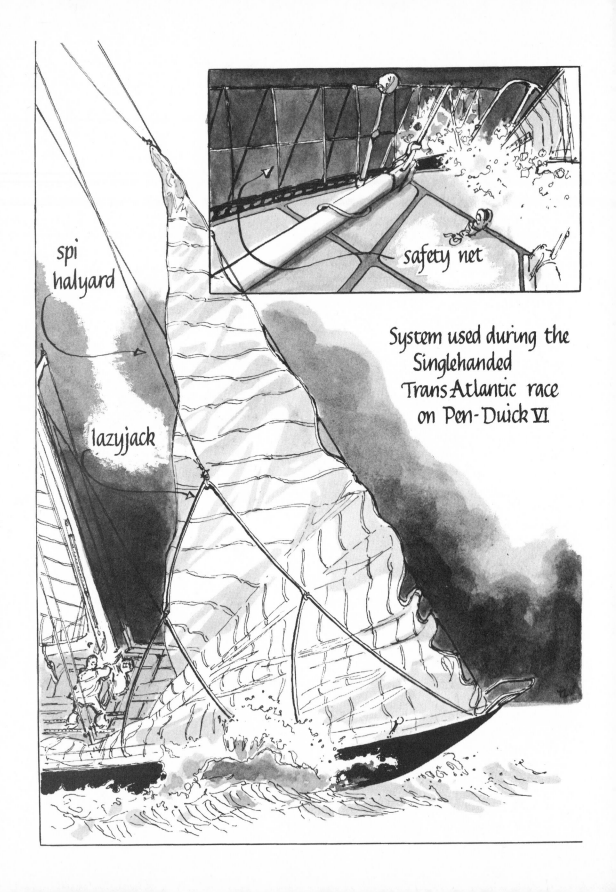

spi
halyard

lazyjack

safety net

System used during the
Singlehanded
TransAtlantic race
on Pen-Duick VI

to pass behind the stay. It is enough then to return the halyard to the head of the new sail just before hoisting. This sounds simple, indeed childishly so, and yet it is incredible the number of crew who contrive to hoist headsails with the halyard twisted. One must supervise and make a few sharp remarks to get them into the habit of carrying out these simple actions, for it is most important always to do this; on a big boat one cannot see high enough up the mast by the light of a hand torch to tell whether the halyard is clear or not. And a twisted halyard is weakened in only a few hours.

Reefing genoa

This sail offers the useful facility of being able to shorten the headsail without changing it. It is easier to take a reef in a genoa than to replace it, and also it saves the cost of two other jibs, and leaves more room in the sail locker.

The reef cringle in the leech must not be too high to allow a sheet to be easily passed through it, as this is the first step when reefing. This auxiliary sheet can either pass through another block on the sheet track or one fixed to the deck; it is made fast to a cleat or a spare winch, but there is no need for it to be tightened. Its only purpose is to secure the reef cringle within reach so that the proper sheets can be shifted to it. The halyard and sheet are slacked off, and the tack cringle for the reef is brought down to the stemhead, where it is attached by a simple rope strop. The sheet is attached and the position of the deck travellers adjusted if necessary. Once the working sheet is set up taut, the temporary one can be removed.

The halyard is set up and belayed, and nothing remains but to tidy up the loose sail. The reef points should be close enough together to prevent the formation of large pockets of water between each one. Generally one does not use a continuous lacing as on the mainsail. The tension on the foot varies considerably (when tacking, or loosening the sheet off the wind), so a lacing would not remain even. Short cords or reef points are therefore needed, either permanently fixed to the reefing eyelets or prepared and kept at hand for the purpose.

Order of reducing sail

There are no rules: it depends on the boat and the balance of the sail plan.

Generally, with most modern sloops or cutters large headsails (of heavier weight) are kept up as long as possible. This is to say that once the heavy genoa or yankee jib is set, shortening sail begins with reefing the main, before changing to smaller headsails.

133

Some ketches begin to carry weather helm when the breeze freshens, and with these one begins by reducing the mizzen or striking it altogether. Others, better balanced, keep their mizzens: if not, they begin to exhibit lee helm. The result would be an inability to point well, because the helmsman has great difficulty in keeping the bow up to the proper course when every wave makes her tend to bear away. That is the case with *Pen Duick VI*, where reduction of sail begins with the mainsail. The order is as follows: the boat carries the heavy no. 2 genoa staysail and the heavy no. 2 yankee jib. One then takes one reef in the main, then the second. Next one changes down to no. 3 yankee, and then the main is lowered altogether. She goes very well to windward with this sail plan. Then one changes to the no. 1 jib and no. 3 staysail, then no. 2 jib and no. 4 staysail, and the mizzen is reefed. But the wind must be a good 50 knots before the mizzen needs to be reefed. Finally one changes to no. 3 jib and takes the second reef on the mizzen. Sail has seldom been reduced any further, but if necessary one would strike the no. 3 jib, and continue under staysail and double-reefed mizzen.

For schooners it is the same thing. A schooner like *Pen Duick III* with two equal masts was like a ketch, and it was always best to begin by shortening the foresail, which was struck altogether before beginning to reduce the headsails. A classic schooner with a large mainsail will begin by reefing that.

The order of sail reduction is therefore above all a matter of the skipper knowing his own boat.

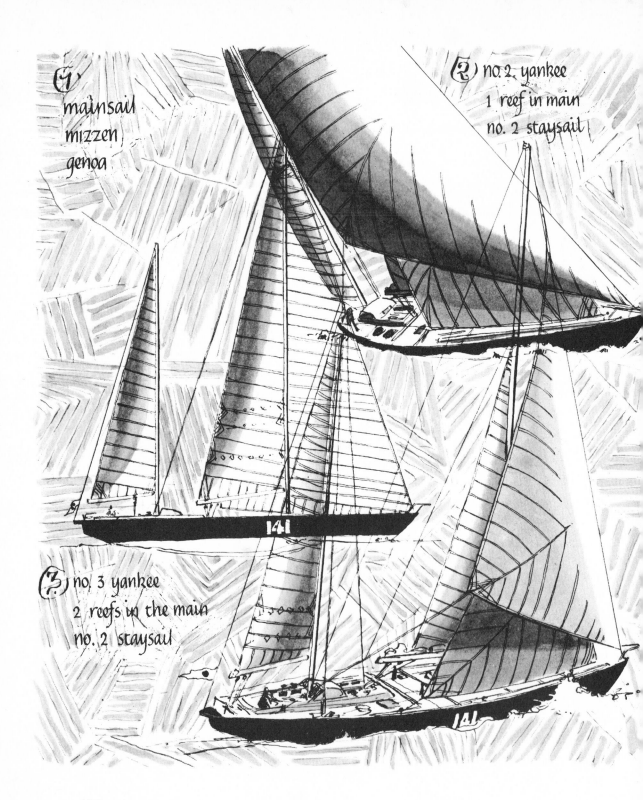

1. mainsail
   mizzen
   genoa

2. no. 2 yankee
   1 reef in main
   no. 2 staysail

3. no. 3 yankee
   2 reefs in the main
   no. 2 staysail

141

141

4. no. 1 jib, then no. 2
mainsail struck
no. 2 staysail, then no. 3

5. 1 reef in mizzen
no. 3 jib
no. 4 staysail

6. 2 reefs in
mizzen

no. 4 staysail

...eduction of
...il aboard
...en-Duick VI

137

Handling in heavy weather

Heavy weather with a fair wind

I believe that with a fair wind fast, light boats can keep going no matter what the conditions. That is the case with boats like *Pen Duick III* or *Pen Duick VI*. During the 1973–4 Round the World Race, particularly on the Cape Town–Sydney leg, *Pen Duick VI* was always able to hold her course and carry plenty of sail. We kept along the 45th parallel for thirteen days, and over those thirteen days our shortest daily run was 261 miles: say an average of 10.9 knots. The wind was never less than 30–35 knots, and the worst squalls reached 70 knots.

At all times the mainsail stayed up, as did the mizzen and often a mizzen staysail. Forward we had at least a big yankee jib downwind and a reasonable sized jib boomed out to windward, but most of the time it was a large or small spinnaker. Under these conditions the boat surfed magnificently, and we were never once pooped. I think that this was because of our speed. Admittedly we were in a race and carried the maximum of sail at all times, with the risk, particularly under spinnaker, of broaching. Sailing like this, always right to the limit, certainly gave us a few nasty frights, but cruising it would have been enough to be content with one knot less, and we would have been perfectly comfortable. A difference of one knot at high speeds represents an enormous difference in the propulsive force, and thus in the sail area needed. We could easily observe this while we were changing sails. Under main and mizzen alone, we did not lose more than two knots. So, accepting a speed of 10 knots instead of 11, the boat would have been rather undercanvassed, with no more risk of broaching, but still with enough speed for safe sailing.

Why is speed a safety factor? There are two reasons. First, a fast boat is overtaken slowly by the waves and the force of their impact, if they strike, is proportionately reduced. Second, high speed is necessary to preserve the efficiency of the rudder. When a wave passes under a boat she will slow down on its rear face and reach minimum speed in the trough of the wave just at the moment when the next wave lifts the stern into the wind, trying to make her yaw, pivoting on her forefoot. If the speed is too low the rudder will not have enough power to counter this yaw, and she will broach-to. If the wave is high and breaking, that can have unpleasant consequences. That, I think, is what happened to *Sayula II* between the Cape of Good Hope and Sydney. According to the crew *Sayula* was sailing on a broad reach in a wind of about 50 knots. She was then only carrying a small jib and small staysail, which is very little. She must therefore have lacked the speed to counteract the yawing effect of the swell, and she ended up being rolled over by a wave with her

a boat braked by towing warps may easily be pooped

masts 20° or 30° below the horizontal, with all the discomforts and damage that that sort of thing involves.

This question of speed is therefore very important, to my mind. That is why I am against towing warps when running. For fear of going too fast, one runs under bare poles. As a result the boat will not steer any more, and to hold her stern-to-wind one streams warps, and indeed anything else of the kind that can be found, such as fenders, chains or spare lines. The boat can then be pooped by each wave. That is the conclusion Bernard Moitessier reached in the South Pacific. *Joshua*'s position had become untenable, so after considerable hesitation Bernard decided to cut away his warps. He was thoroughly satisfied with the result.

Now why did he want to limit his speed? Because his nightmare, the result no doubt of having read it somewhere, was of being pitchpoled, that is turned end over end. He imagined it happening in the following manner: the boat begins to surf like a cannonball down the face of a wave, overtakes the wave that is driving her on, and digs her bow into the back of the preceding one. I do not believe that this is possible. With a boat like *Pen Duick VI* that surfs very well – which was certainly not the case with *Joshua* – and maintains maximum speed with a full racing crew, we never overtook a wave in the southern latitudes. And that is despite some splendid toboggan rides, with the speedometer against its stop at 24 knots. It was very spectacular, but the driving wave always overtook us, because these huge rollers travel at very high speeds. It was in fact that factor that allowed us to surf very much faster than would have been possible in other waters, even in the same wind and carrying the same canvas. There is a mathematical relationship between the height of a wave and its speed, and that is why, even during our most spectacular surfs, I never had a moment's worry that we would dig our bow into the wave ahead.

If light boats capable of planing well are happy in high following seas, it can be quite a different matter for heavy ones, with a strictly limited maximum speed. It has often happened that some boats take so many seas over the stern that they prefer to heave-to. Then one must choose the moment to luff up with great care.

Heaving-to or lying a-hull

It can happen that the wind is so strong and the sea so heavy that the boat can no longer make headway against the wind without risk of damage, as the shock of each wave becomes too severe. It also happens, in very heavy weather, that certain heavy boats risk being swept by seas on downwind courses. Finally, it may be that for a variety of other reasons one decides to stop battling

142

against bad weather. Thus, when cruising one may heave-to even if the boat is still capable of standing up to the assault of the sea, in order to save wear on the equipment or rest the crew. In the Singlehanded Transatlantic Race of 1976, during the fifth depression I had met, which proved to be the worst, I lay a-hull so as not to risk the loss of my mizzen. Since I had no self-steering, this sail had become essential to balance the boat so that she would sail with the helm lashed. In spite of the severe conditions the boat could have continued to make progress, but it was not certain that the mizzen would stand it. The least tear in a wind like that would have meant that the whole sail would have been in shreds before it could be got down, and quite irreparable by the means available on board. That was a risk I could not afford.

In all these cases, there is only one solution: heave-to.

Running under bare poles can often be more comfortable, but if the destination is to windward and one is therefore going to have to beat, running off downwind can cost a considerably amount of ground. It may also be that there is not much sea-room to leeward, or that running would be dangerous with your boat.

One will either lie a-hull under bare poles, or heave-to under small storm sails: the choice of method depends on the characteristics of the boat. A light displacement type, with a very short keel and good stability built into the hull shape, is the ideal boat to lie a-hull, that is without any sail. I think the best example of this type of boat is *Pen Duick III*. In January 1968 we were caught in a storm aboard her between New Caledonia and the Loyalty Islands while on passage to Nouméa. According to the weather bulletins the wind was about 100 knots in our area. We were sailing hard on the wind carrying nothing but a small staysail, and the wind had already passed its maximum. We were pointing well, and it is comforting to reflect that if we had been near a lee shore we would have been able to make an offing, as long as the sails held together. (If that staysail had blown out, we still had the storm jib which was brand new because it had never been used. This sail is so heavy that it is hardly conceivable for it to fail. It is essential to have such a sail aboard, even if it is never used, because in extreme conditions it might save the boat and crew. On *Pen Duick VI* I even have two identical storm jibs that have never been set, but I would certainly never be without them.) Naturally it was extremely uncomfortable. The boat was heeled at an acute angle, and slammed deafeningly into the very bad sea. The waves had not yet had time to build up to a great amplitude, but they were very steep, close together and breaking. What with the rain, torrential as usual in a cyclone, the clouds of spindrift torn off the wave crests by the wind, and the gouts of water thrown up by the bows, the air was so full of humidity that from time to time one breathed in so

Pen-Duick III
- light displacement
- short keel
- good stability of hull shape
- the ideal boat
  for lying a-hull

much water that one was left gasping for air. There was no question of looking to windward, so viciously did the spray drive into the eyes. What was the point in going on thrashing to windward in such conditions? In any case it was out of the question in that weather to try to beat through the coral heads to reach Nouméa. We had already lost the mainsail right at the beginning of the blow, and it wasn't worth risking blowing out the staysail as well. So I decided to strike it. The boat was now under bare poles, and suddenly everything seemed to moderate. We knew very well that the wind was still just as strong, and the spectacle of the sea completely white with spray, with fountains of spindrift swirling into the sky, was there to remind us. But apart from that it did not feel like bad weather any more. Thanks to her light displacement, her small

144

wetted surface and her narrow fin keel, *Pen Duick III* drifted abeam very quickly, at about three knots, so that the shock of the waves was deadened, and not one succeeded in smashing against the hull. The wake which she left to windward must have helped to flatten them and prevent them from breaking. Thanks to her stable shape, she did not roll her rails under. The pressure of the wind in the rigging gave her a moderate heel. Life on board became perfectly comfortable. The helm was lashed a-lee. There was 60 miles of searoom downwind before the first land. We went to sleep and waited for things to calm down.

Pen Duick VI, thanks to her light displacement and narrow keel, also lies a-hull well, but with less comfort than *Pen Duick III*. With her rounded hull section she rolls heavily, and the rolling can sometimes become trying, even

heavy displacement, long keel with little ballast: this boat will suffer badly lying a-hull

capsizing couple

145

though there is no serious risk of damage or injury. One still feels oneself to be perfectly safe.

The worst boat for lying a-hull is one of heavy displacement with a long and lightly ballasted keel. Her keel and the depth of the hull offer considerable resistance to sideways drift, and reduce this to negligible proportions. The waves are then able to break against her, and it is easy to see that the force of the impact on the freeboard, and the lateral resistance of the submerged section, create a couple that tends to knock down or capsize the boat, the more easily according to the lack of ballast. Such boats should therefore heave-to under sail.

In heaving-to the boat must be brought to about 60° off the wind, so as to take the seas three-quarters on the bow. There must not be too much forward speed, to avoid increasing the impact of the waves, but a certain minimum is needed to prevent the hull being thrown backwards by the waves, which no rudder will stand up to. To achieve this aim the sail must obviously be chosen in the light of the boat, her balance and the sail plan.

Two-masted rigs, with their horizontally extended sail plans, are the best for stable heaving-to under sail. Aft, a yawl will carry a mizzen, and a ketch a reefed mizzen; as for schooners, even the fully reefed mainsail is likely to be too big and a storm trysail will probably be needed. Forward, one will hoist a storm jib, which is used to control the speed by sheeting it more or less into the wind. By adjusting the sheets of the after and headsails, one should be able to achieve a gentle forward speed three-quarters on to the sea.

Sloops and cutters are less stable in balance, and there is a good chance that their bows will fall off to leeward at each wave. There is thus even a risk that they may sometimes find themselves broadside-on to the sea at times. They do well to have a storm sail cut as long in the foot as possible, with a sheeting point as far aft as the deck plan allows. Cutters have the advantage of being able to hank their storm foresail onto the inner stay, which reduces the tendency to fall off. A sloop, to avoid getting broadside-on, has only the resource of keeping a higher speed to prevent this problem, but she will then slam into the seas that much more.

It is useful to have a **storm trysail** aboard all boats, even ketches and yawls which heave-to under mizzen. After all, that can always blow out. I think it is useful to be able to fix the trysail clew to the boom, which avoids having to rig separate sheets. But it should be able to be set without the boom, in case that should be broken.

I do not feel that I should discuss the weight of sailcloth that should be used for storm sails, and yet perhaps I must. Once at Marseilles, with the *mistral* blowing 50 to 60 knots, I saw boats returning to harbour with the clew

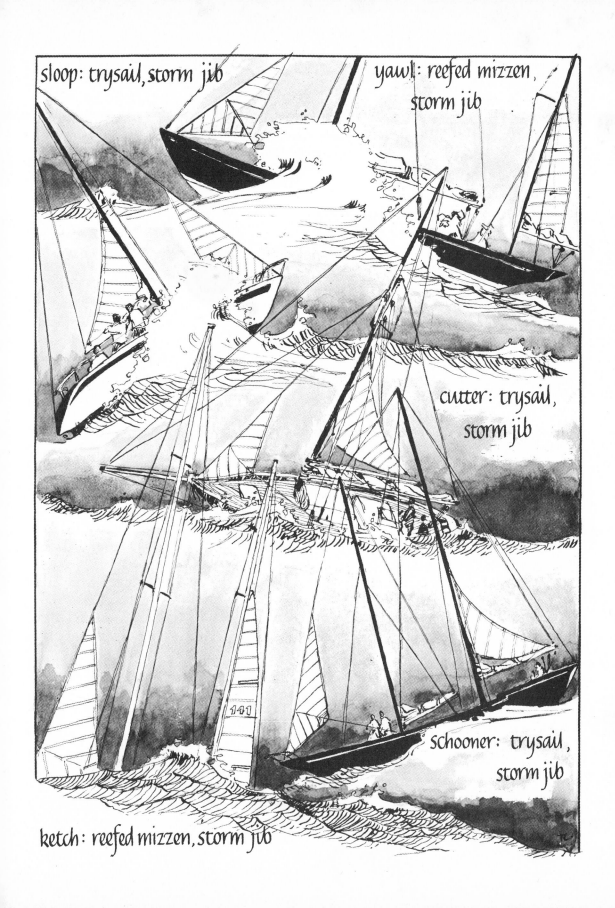

sloop: trysail, storm jib

yawl: reefed mizzen, storm jib

cutter: trysail, storm jib

Schooner: trysail, storm jib

ketch: reefed mizzen, storm jib

cringles ripped out of their storm jibs. It is criminal of a sailmaker to supply a boat with a storm jib or trysail that is capable of tearing. They should be indestructible: the survival of the boat and crew may one day depend upon it.

The sea anchor

At the risk of greatly shocking numerous people, I have to say that I think it is always a dead loss. If hove-to with a sea anchor streamed over the bow, with a small sail astern or none at all, the boat will be thrown backwards and the rudder, unless it is incredibly heavily built and fastened, will be smashed. Streaming it over the stern, we are brought back to the arguments about towing warps or other things, which have already been discussed.

It can only be useful in one case: to put off the fatal hour when a boat is thrown up on a lee shore. The weather may be too bad for this boat to be able to make headway and claw off, or damage may have made it impossible for her to sail to windward. The sea anchor will greatly reduce the speed of drift, and to that extent postpone the moment when she strikes. During the extra time the wind may change or help may arrive.

The sea anchor should be attached by a nylon warp and a chain. The elasticity of the nylon and the weight of the chain reduce the snubbing. The chain should be at the boat end, because the nylon will not stand up to the chafing in the fairlead. And unless you have absolute confidence in your deck fittings for mooring, do not hesitate to use the foot of the mast as a samson post.

148

Jury rigs

There are two major occurrences which necessitate improvising a rig which will enable the boat to be got under way and brought to a harbour. They are the loss of the rudder, and dismasting.

In theory it is possible to steer a boat without the use of a rudder, by playing with the sheets of the headsails and after sails. Although this is easy enough to achieve with a sailing dinghy, it is not the same at all when dealing with a cruising yacht, unless it is one with very good directional stability and a long keel. A boat with a short keel and a separate rudder a long way aft of the keel has good directional stability as long as the rudder is there, but none at all once it is out of action. To steer a boat of this kind by the use of the sheets only is virtually impossible.

This type of accident happened to me aboard *Pen Duick II* in 1966, during the Bermuda–Copenhagen Race. We were 450 miles south of St Pierre and Miquelon, the French islands just south of Newfoundland, sailing on a broad reach with the big spinnaker and the mizzen spinnaker set, and the boat was steering easily without the need for any heavy pressure on the helm. Suddenly I felt everything go slack, and the boat began to luff. The designer had not made the rudder fittings heavy enough, and after a good many thousand miles it had ended up by fracturing on a day when no special strain was being put on it.

We immediately knocked up a sort of steering oar from a spinnaker pole and two cabin floorboards. These two small plywood panels were placed in a V at one end of the spar. A few turns of line served to hold them in the

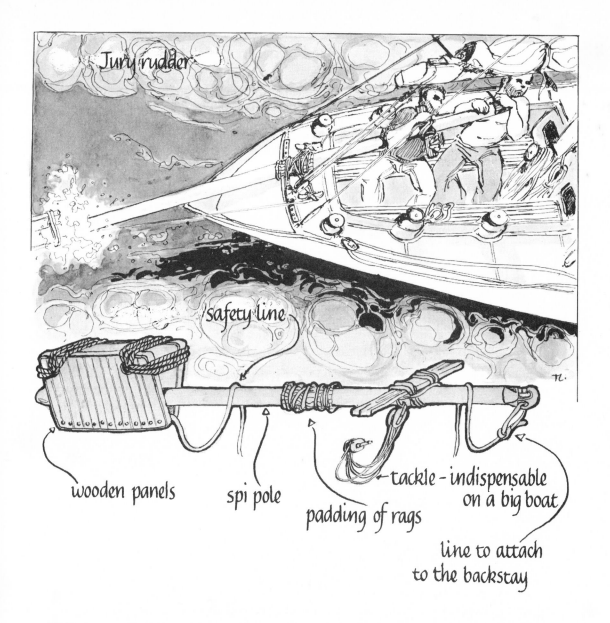

Jury rudder

safety line

wooden panels   spi pole   tackle - indispensable on a big boat

padding of rags

line to attach to the backstay

V shape, and another lashed them to the pole, making use of the holes designed for lifting them out by. In this way we avoided having to saw and drill, and all the material could later be returned to its original use. A crew member who thought little of this arrangement wanted to cut a slot in the afterdeck, saw the mizzen boom in half, and so on. A great deal of damage for a very complicated system which nobody else could understand. Our simple arrangement didn't work so badly. We had lashed a piece of wood at right angles to the pole at its other end, and this served to keep the panels vertical, as they tended to twist flat on top of the water. The part of the pole that was lashed to the afterdeck was well padded with rags to prevent abrasion of the wood. A line kept it from sliding aft. The only inconvenience was that we could not exceed 5 knots, because over that speed, even with two steering, the oar was too exhausting to cope with. We therefore reduced sail to keep below that speed, and in that manner reached St Pierre in five days with no bother.

It is very clear that *Pen Duick II*'s moderate size (6.5 tons displacement) made the thing much easier. On a big boat it would be different. I think that one would stick to the easily realized principle of the steering oar. The work would be more complicated, because it would be necessary to fix sufficiently large surfaces to the shaft, and the assembly would have to be solid as it would be subject to considerable strain. The method of construction would depend on what was available aboard. When he lost his rudder during his race round the world, Olivier de Kersauson on *Kriter II* made one by fixing aluminium sheets to a spinnaker pole. This could be done with bolts, but if a pop-riveter is carried this is clearly the simplest method to achieve a good job. Unfortunately it is not every boat that carries sheet metal.

Once the oar has been got together, the weight of the pole, the pressure needed to manœuvre the boat, and the height that the tiller end of the oar projects above deck level all combine to make it impossible for the helmsman to steer by hand. It is necessary to rig a tackle on each side. Unfortunately these will pull downwards, tending to raise the rudder end out of the water, so the inner end of the oar must be supported by a line lashed to the backstay.

As long as the accident does not happen when you are near a lee shore, do not think that all is lost if this happens to you. No Mayday calls or rockets: try to get out of the situation through your own resources. Remember that tows from commercial vessels generally prove catastrophic for a yacht. A cargo ship cannot spare the time (or may not be able to go at low speeds) to tow you slowly enough for safety, and in any case there is every chance that she will collide with you while the towline is being passed. Unless the sea is completely flat, which is rare, your hull and rigging will suffer severely. If you want to escape with the least possible damage, get out of it yourself.

The same thing goes for a dismasting. Have patience, take whatever time is needed, but get back to port using your own resources.

There are two possible situations: that in which a stump of mast is left, and that in which the mast has broken off at deck level, or was stepped on deck and has gone overboard.

The first case may be more favourable to your chances of being able in the end to set a reasonable area of sail, but you may have a lot of trouble securing

152

the upper part of the mast or getting rid of it. With aluminium masts the break is seldom complete, and the two halves remain joined by a strip of metal. Even if the break is complete the internal halyards will hold the two parts together. One can try cutting them, but usually they are jammed at the fracture point and still hold.

If the break is below the level of the lowest spreaders, but fairly high above the deck, it is likely that the lower part of the mast will break off at deck level in due course. This is what happened to us with *Pen Duick VI* off the Glénans. A stump about 5 to 6 metres high remained standing above the deck, and the whole upper part of the mast was held by the internal halyards. All this rigging lying in the water alongside prevented the boat from drifting and formed a sea anchor, exercising a powerful lateral pull on the top of the lower section of the mast. This, having no shrouds to support it, finished by breaking off just above the deck at the level of the exits for the halyards, which weaken the construction. This happened after only a few minutes, while we were still busy freeing the mainsail from the boom. In these circumstances it is important to bear in mind that this second fracture is likely, and to avoid having anyone working in a position where something will land on his head if it happens. It is also unwise to climb the mast to work on the fracture until the lower part has been supported in some way.

If the break takes place above the spreaders the mast will remain well supported by the lower shrouds. The break may be high enough for the masthead to hang above deck level, in which case it will swing dangerously and must be secured firmly along the lower part of the mast. I experienced this type of dismasting when I was at the helm of the 12 Metre *Constellation* in a violent squall off Newport. The masthead came to just above the deck, which made it easy to secure, and there was no sea to speak of.

If the masthead is in the water, then according to the length of mast over the side it may or may not be possible to bring it back on deck. It will be necessary to try to detach the mainsail from the mast. This may well be difficult, because someone will certainly have to climb up to cut off the boltrope or the slide seizings along the lower part of the mast, to enable the upper part of the sail to be slid towards the masthead. If this is in the water recovery of the mainsail may be difficult, or even impossible. It is valuable to be able to recover the top section of the mast, because it will enable a jury mast to be rigged high enough to set a useful area of sail. In bad weather an improvement in conditions will probably have to be awaited before someone can be sent up to work on the break.

If the break is far enough above the spreaders somebody has the fun of climbing up there to fix a permanent block to support a halyard for the bosun's

154

1. amusing little job of fixing temporary block for bosun's chair

2. fixing a block more permanently

chair. Once that is done the worst is over. It may have to be done in two stages: fixing a temporary block to allow the chair to be used to install a second one more permanently. The second block must be fixed only to the standing part of the mast, whereas the first lash-up, because it will be done in a hurry and must not slip, will probably pass over the fracture itself.

Once the bosun's chair is solidly anchored, it becomes easy to get rid of everything that is holding the two parts of the mast together. The halyards are cut, or disengaged in one piece if they will run, and any metal still joining the two parts cut through with a hacksaw. Before beginning, remember to set up a block and a line supporting the upper part of the mast, made fast so as to prevent it falling onto the deck when it is released. With this, it can be lowered gently. Another preliminary is to remove the spreaders. They will be used again, unless the mast has two sets, in which case it will probably be the upper ones that are reused.

Normally the masthead will be brought aboard aft. In that way the whole of the deck area between the stern pulpit and the foot of the mast is available to work from. If the masthead has been recovered onto the foredeck, it must be turned with the broken end aft if necessary.

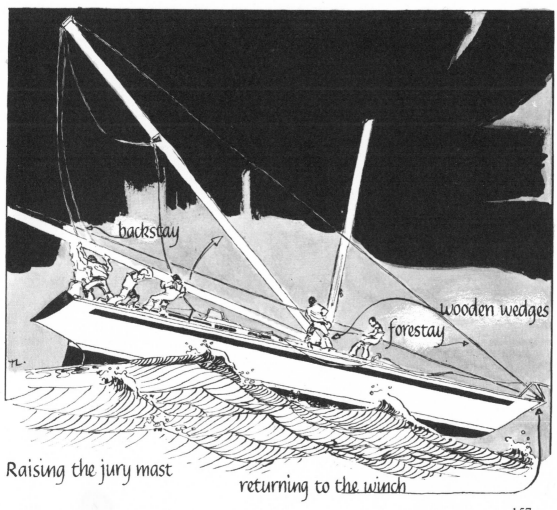

backstay

wooden wedges

forestay

Raising the jury mast

returning to the winch

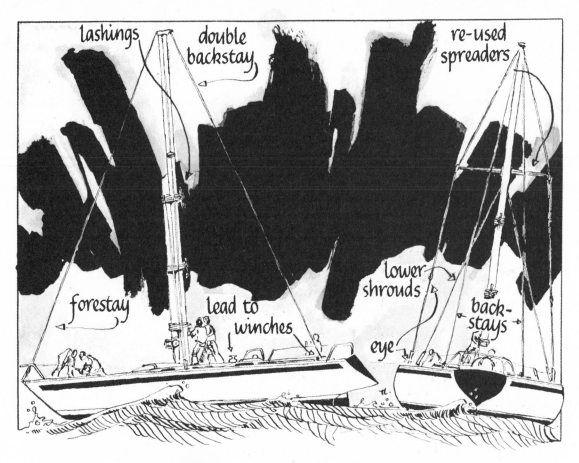

In either case the technique of re-rigging is the same. First of all new shrouds and halyards must be set up. Next, the lower end of the broken-off section is wedged against the bottom of the stump, using either a lashing or wooden wedges. The fore and backstays will pass through blocks at the stemhead and stern respectively. The backstays may be double, with each stay passing through a block on the quarter. According to the situation, either the forestay or the backstays are winched in, letting out the opposite stay or stays as needed. If only one backstay has been rigged the mast will have to be supported laterally by a line at each side. Once the mast is vertical, if its height is satisfactory, things can be left at that. Set up the stays good and tight, and adjust the shrouds.

If the height is insufficient, one can hoist the detached section up the lower mast, as one does the topmast in a gaff-rigger. This operation will involve a good deal of work, but it will be worth the trouble if one is a long way from port. The end of a line is fixed to one side of the lower masthead, and a block to the other. To do this holes may have to be drilled to allow wire rope to

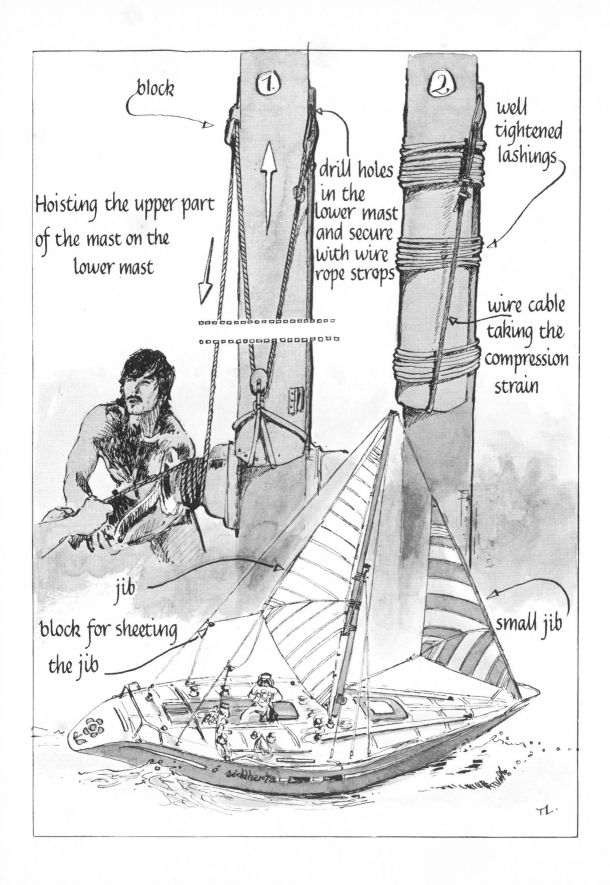

block

①

Hoisting the upper part
of the mast on the
lower mast

drill holes
in the
lower mast
and secure
with wire
rope strops

②

well
tightened
lashings

wire cable
taking the
compression
strain

jib

block for sheeting
the jib

small jib

be used for securing. Another block is fixed to the lower end of what is to be the topmast. The line, whether fibre or wire, thus runs from one side of the top of the lower mast down and through the block at the foot of the topmast, then up and through the block at the lower masthead, and finally through a block on deck from where it is led to a winch. Slackening its stays, and the lateral lines if any, as needed, and using a winch to haul in on this tackle, one can thus raise the upper part of the mast. If you are worried that the lifting line or blocks may not stand up to the compression strains that will be set up when sail is set, you can add a good lashing of wire rope between the head of the lower mast and the foot of the topmast. The hoisting line is then slackened to allow the lashing to take up the tension. The two parts of the mast

Jury rig of Pen-Duick VI
after her first dismasting

spinnaker poles

are bound together with a seizing, well tightened by a 'garrotte' – Spanish wind-lass – a bar or marlinspike passed through one of the turns and then twisted round as often as needed. The stays are tightened well and the shrouds adjusted: a new eye will have to be put in the end of each so that the rigging screws can be used again. This can be done by using cable clamps (of which it is always useful to have a small stock aboard), or if there are none by seizings, in the traditional fashion, which will have to be well made if they are not going to slip. If the rigging screws were swaged onto the ends of the wire it will have to be cut and rejoined to the proper length by making two eyes, one inside the other.

On this mast one will now be able to set a small jib forward, and aft perhaps the reefed main, if it has been recovered in good condition, or otherwise the trysail or even a jib. In the latter case the clew will set very high, and it will have to be sheeted through a block lashed to the backstay, or better yet to

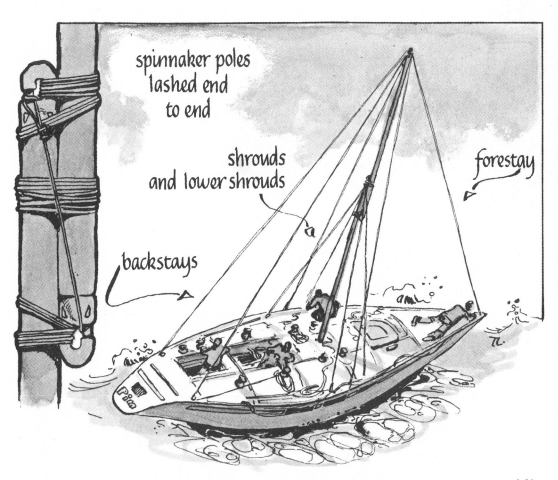

both the backstays if there are two. One can also set a jib so that the luff serves as its leech (i.e. hoisted by the tack), but the performance will be very poor.

If the whole mast has gone over the side and nothing can be recovered, which is unfortunately often the case when big boats are dismasted, one can then rig a mast either from the boom if it is still aboard, or from the spinnaker poles, which on modern designs are often longer than the main boom. That is what we did aboard *Pen Duick VI*. For this, one end of each pole is attached to the toerail, and the free ends fastened together with a good lashing. Fore and backstays are rigged, and two halyard blocks lashed to the joined ends. We were able in this way to set the storm jib forward, and the trysail aft, set luff downwards. Of course this was very little, but luckily as *Pen Duick VI* was ketch rigged we also had the mizzen mast which gave us a good sail area off the wind thanks to the mizzen staysail.

On a sloop, the amount of sail one could set on this rig would not be likely to be enough. One can then lash the two poles end to end. A lashing through the two end-fittings takes up the compression strain, and a seizing well tightened by a spike holds them one against the other. The head of the lower pole is stayed with an inner forestay or two shrouds pulling forwards, and two lower shrouds pulling aft. According to its design, one may or may not have to remove the fitting from the lower end of the lower pole. There is no doubt that this will be a fragile rig, and it will have to be treated with great care in any sort of breeze.

Man overboard
manoeuvres

The first essential is to keep cool, so as to be able to carry out the drill in order and methodically.

(1) Throw the lifebuoy with its marker pole, if one is carried aboard.

(2) Detail a crew member to watch the person in the water. He should not take his eyes off him for a second, as nothing is harder to pick out than a little dot in the midst of the waves, once one has lost it.

(3) At the same time as (1) and (2), the helmsman quickly brings the boat onto a heading at right angles to the true wind.

(4) Proceed on this course for a few boat's lengths, then bear away onto a downwind course.

(5) Gybe, then luff onto a reach, heading for a point downwind of the man.

(6) To come up into the wind without aiming straight at the person, one must have gone slightly past him. Aim for an upwind leg shorter than that necessary to stop the boat. That way the boat will carry way to weather of the man.

(7) Tack, keeping the jib backed, so as to finish up hove-to to weather of him. Then drift down on him broadside-on, playing the mainsheet if necessary.

The person must not be approached downwind, because of the risk of killing him or knocking him out with a blow from the stem as the boat pitches. It is best to finish the manœuvre hove-to to windward of him, because the boat heeling towards him makes it easier to get him back aboard. One has often seen cases of people being unable to get back aboard, even with the help of the crew. With an athletic crew there is no problem, but if they are physically

164

out of condition one must expect that they will be unable to haul an overweight and exhausted colleague back aboard. It is then necessary, without wasting time and getting uselessly exhausted, to take a halyard (that for the spinnaker will be the best adapted) and clip it to his harness if he is wearing one, or to a rope passed under his arms and tied into a loop. He will still need to have enough strength left to keep his arms down to stop the loop from slipping. He is then hoisted by means of the halyard winch. One can also pass him the bosun's chair, provided he is capable of getting it under his feet so that he can get his legs through: this requires that he is reasonably at ease in the water.

During the manœuvre it is vital always to know where the person is. If one loses sight of him, he may never be found again if there is any sea running. It is therefore very advisable to have good position marking equipment aboard: for daytime, a float with a flagpole attached to the buoy, and for use at night a powerful automatic light, also attached to the buoy. It takes time to get the buoy over the side, and if the boat is travelling fast it will fall some distance from the man. If the wind is strong it will drift faster than the person,

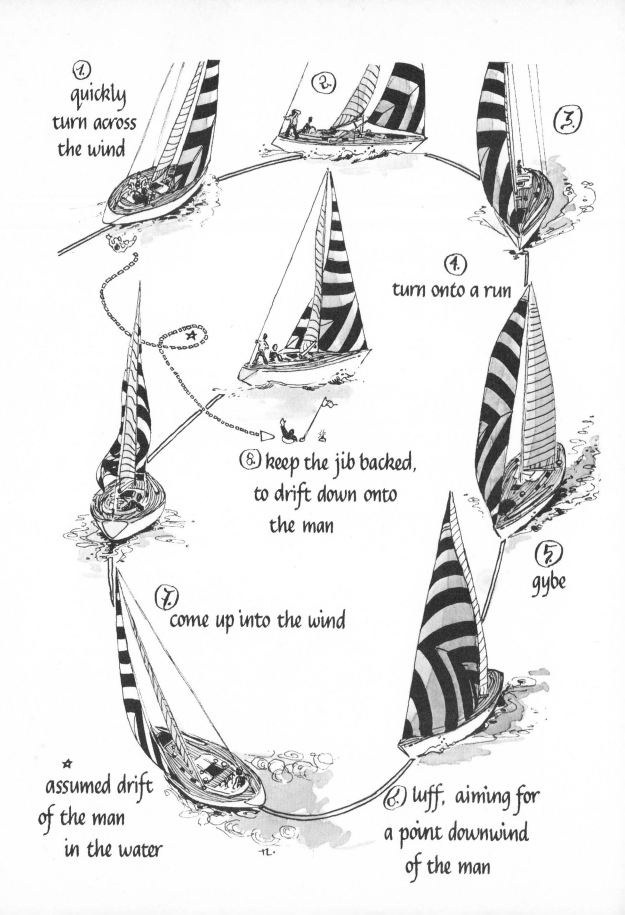

1. quickly turn across the wind

2.

3.

4. turn onto a run

8. keep the jib backed, to drift down onto the man

5. gybe

7. come up into the wind

★ assumed drift of the man in the water

6. luff, aiming for a point downwind of the man

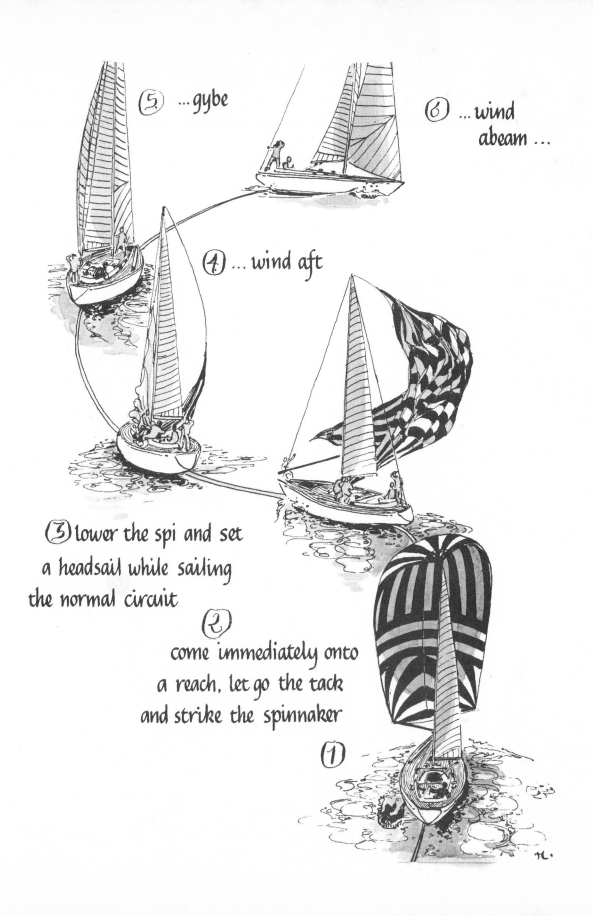

⑤ ...gybe

⑥ ...wind
abeam ...

④ ... wind aft

③ lower the spi and set
a headsail while sailing
the normal circuit

②
come immediately onto
a reach, let go the tack
and strike the spinnaker

①

and he will be unable to swim to it. A small drogue should therefore be added, to limit the buoy's rate of drift.

The manœuvre may miss its target, but still have the boat pass within a few metres of the man. A line must therefore be ready to throw to the casualty in case he can catch it and has the strength to hold on. If so he can be brought alongside without the need to get under way and go round again.

The trickiest situation is of course when running under spinnaker in a good breeze. The boat would cover too much distance if one waited until it was handed before luffing. The guy should be let out right away to let the pole swing forward, while at the same time the helmsman turns broadside-on to the wind. The spinnaker is then handed, the pole dropped and a new headsail set, so that the manœuvre can be completed hove-to. During this period, the usual little circuit will have been completed: run, gybe, reach.

Man-overboard drill must be practised, exercising by recovering a buoy thrown overboard. It must even be done in bad weather, to avoid being taken by surprise and stopping too short on the final leg. With the wind ahead in

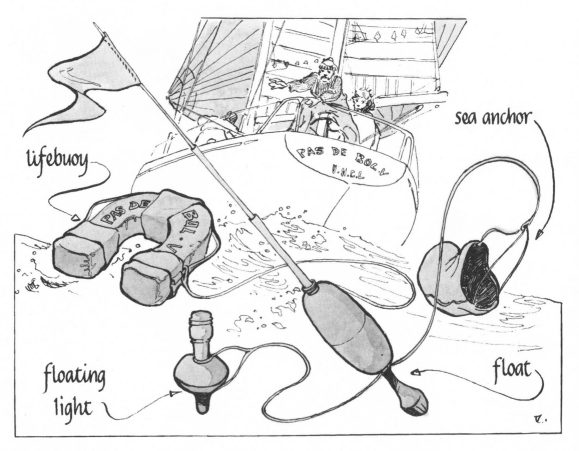

lifebuoy

sea anchor

floating
light

float

a fresh wind and a rough sea, it is surprising how short the stopping distance becomes. Unfortunately, in heavy weather one hesitates to carry out training exercises, and in the end there is a risk of never getting around to it, which is a great pity.

Towing

There are two methods of towing a boat: from the bow or alongside. Towing alongside is best in confined spaces, as it enables tight turns to be made, including turning on the spot, and above all it allows way to be got off the tow quickly so that it can be stopped in a short distance. This method should therefore be the one adopted when manœuvring in port, as long as the towing vessel has enough power. With too little power the pair will be unmanageable, so an auxiliary yacht for instance probably will not be able to manœuvre when secured alongside another of similar size whose motor has broken down.

The towing vessel should be secured to the after end of the tow alongside. This is important if good manœuvrability is to be achieved. Clearly, if the rudder of the towing yacht is to be effective it must be level with the stern of the tow, for it is the one which controls the pair, because it gets the flow from the propeller. In practice, one can steer with the tiller of the tow lashed amidships. The towing boat should tie on forward with a bow line and bow spring, and aft with a breastrope. So that the boats do not shift too far along each other when the towing boat changes from going ahead to reverse, these warps must be hauled good and taut. If they cannot be led to winches to do this, the bow line should be set up as taut as possible by hand, and then the slack taken up on the stern warp and spring while the engine goes astern. Do not forget to use plenty of good fenders, as the pressure between the two hulls can be considerable.

When manœuvring, allowance must be made for the wheel effect of the propeller or propellers of the towing boat, unless she is so powerful that the

172

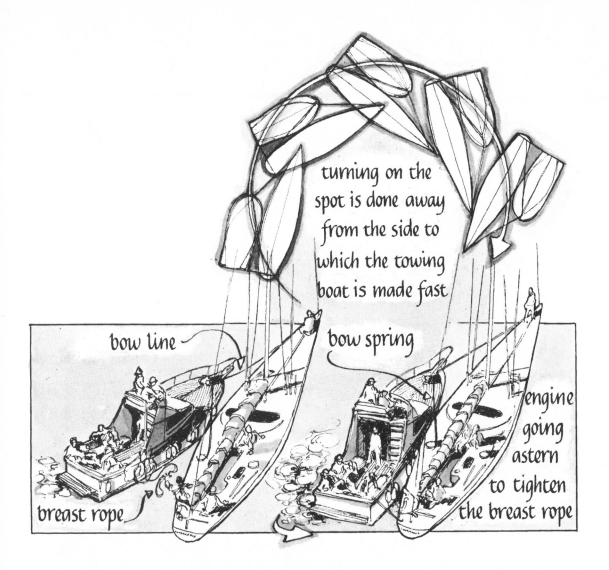

turning on the spot is done away from the side to which the towing boat is made fast

bow line

bow spring

breast rope

engine going astern to tighten the breast rope

effect of the boat alongside is negligible. In particular, turning on the spot can only be done to the side on which the towed boat is secured. The tug, thanks to her propeller effect, will pull her stern away from the side by which it is made fast, and when she goes astern the turn will continue in the same direction. One must always pay close attention to the powerful action of the wheel effect in all manœuvres, when the towing boat's engine is going astern. According to the manœuvre intended, it will therefore often be important to avoid securing the towing boat on one side or the other.

Towing alongside is not recommended at sea, because even in the least chop the fenders will come under unreasonable strain. At sea, therefore, one always tows by the bow. The only problems with tows of this kind are likely to arise

173

in bad weather. In such conditions do not hesitate to use a very long hawser. If the tow is likely to last a long time, nylon rope will not stand up to the constant friction through the fairleads of the tug and the towed boat. It must therefore be replaced at each end by a length of chain or wire rope. If the deck fittings do not seem to be strong enough, the masts must be used to take the pull. That poses no problems for the towed boat, but aboard the tug the chain must be led round from the mast to the after fairlead in such a way that it does not foul the superstructure nor get in the way of manœuvring if the towing vessel is under sail. For this, it is enough to secure it by lashings to three or four strong points. As the chain has no elasticity it will not work and so these lashings will not chafe.

Passing a towline under sail in a breeze and with a sea running can be a tricky business. I once had to take a motor cruiser in tow while sailing with a wind of 25 to 30 knots and a big sea. Our electricity had failed, which meant that we could not start the engine. We could not come head-to-wind at low speed to pass the warp, because we would have been stopped almost instantly by the wind and sea, and the risk of collision would then be very great. I therefore approached on a reach, steering well to leeward of the motor cruiser. I then rounded up onto a closehauled course, but without sheeting in the sails. This way the boat slowed down sharply but remained under control. The genoa prevented the warp being thrown from the lee side of the foredeck, and the crewman in charge was placed about amidships. The problem, in view of the length of *Pen Duick VI*, was that while we travelled half a boat's length (at low speed), the cruiser herself, drifting fast, was making off downwind at quite a speed. Luckily the catchers were adroit, and caught the end of the warp neatly. It would not have been possible to pass closer: I gather that the sight of *Pen Duick*'s bow climbing high out of the sea and falling back so close to windward of them was one to be remembered, not to mention the genoa sheet cracking like a whip above their heads.

Always bear in mind that for a yacht to be towed by a cargo vessel is extremely risky. In almost every instance the yacht suffers severe damage, and often, in any case, the captain of the cargo ship refuses to take the yacht in tow, offering instead where danger exists to take the crew aboard.

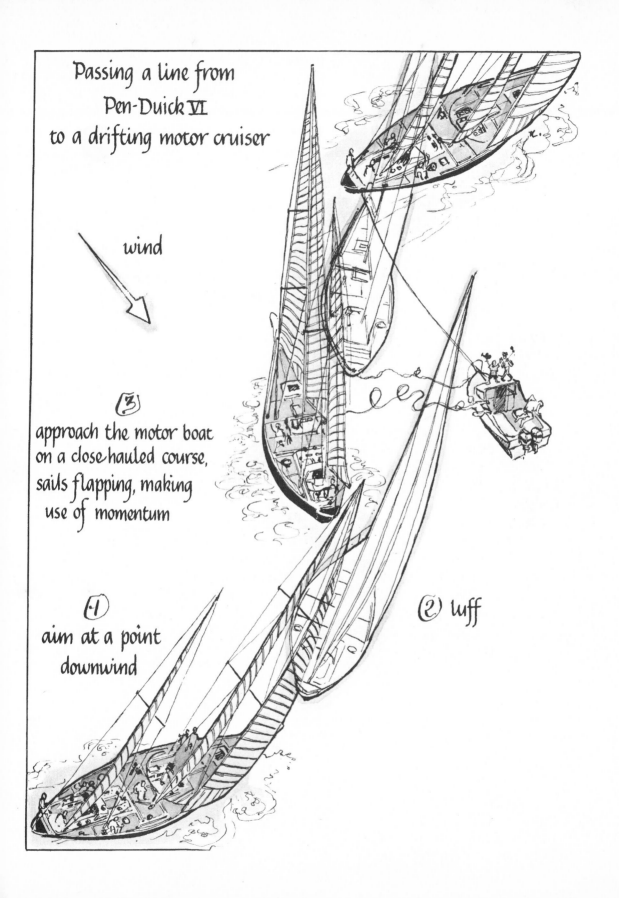

Passing a line from
Pen-Duick VI
to a drifting motor cruiser

wind

③
approach the motor boat
on a close-hauled course,
sails flapping, making
use of momentum

② luff

①
aim at a point
downwind

Everyday seamanship

To do things properly, it is important to know a few knots. But do not waste time struggling to learn the multiplicity of complicated knots described in the seamanship manuals, which are enough to dishearten any beginner from the start. There are really only four that must be known, but you must be able to make them perfectly. There are still too many people about who pretend to know how to sail a boat, but find themselves embarrassed when they have to make something fast (there are even more among the motor cruising fraternity).

I always remember arriving at the Spanish port of San Sebastian, aboard a French yacht on which I was crewing. It must have been a good few years ago, because I was in my very first ocean racing season. A warp had to be sent ashore, so two of us jumped into the dinghy (at that period, rigid tenders were obligatory for ocean racing). As the youngster of the crew I took the oars and the other, a gentleman who had been sailing for years, installed himself in the stern with the end of the warp, which was being paid out from on board. I put him ashore on the ladder with his warp. However, he had never been able to make fast to a ring, and in the end a Spaniard had to come to his assistance. It was a fishermen's feast day, and every quay was black with onlookers. I was absolutely mortified, telling myself that this whole crowd must have been given a rotten opinion of French yachtsmen. Even so, this incident had no unfortunate consequences apart from that moment of shame, which still has not passed, in spite of what they say. But often serious accidents can result from a badly secured mooring, or a knot that has not been made quickly enough.

180

Probably the most commonly used knot is the **bowline**. One really does use it all the time. That is the one that that crewman should have known in San Sebastian. It is used to make a fixed loop at the end of a warp which is to be put over a bollard. It is also used to attach jibsheets, at one end of a sail tie to make a running knot, and on a thousand other occasions. The advantages of this knot are its security and the ease with which it can be untied, even if it has been under heavy strain. But it still needs to have been well made, which means that someone has taken the trouble to tighten it well by hand. Too often one sees crew make this knot without taking that precaution: as a result, it can slip before tightening itself, or come undone, if for instance it has been tied to a clew that thrashes about before the sheet has been tightened. There is even the danger, which does sometimes happen though admittedly rarely, that it will jam, and then once it has been under strain it can only be undone by a quarter of an hour's work with a mallet and spike. So no botched bowlines: there as elsewhere in sailing one must preserve a taste for work well done and well finished. Taking care of what some people might

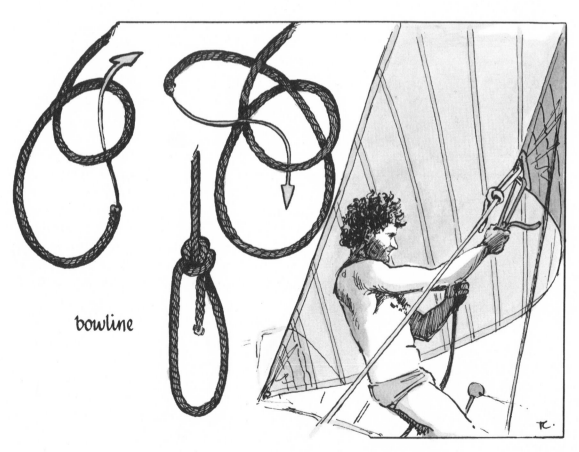

bowline

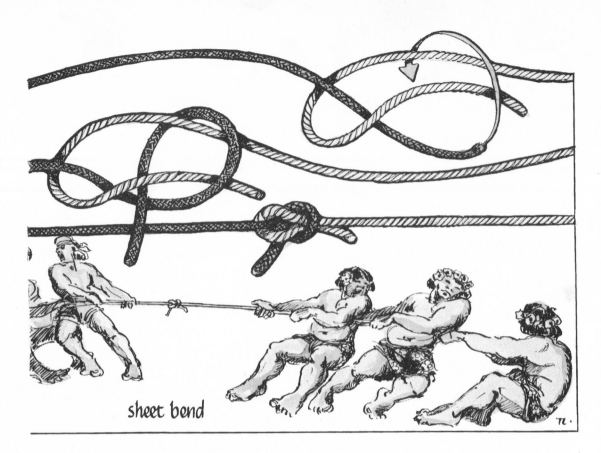

sheet bend

regard as details, but which are in fact very important matters, can save an awful lot of trouble in the end.

The **sheet bend** is used to join two ropes. Some people use the reef knot for this purpose, but this should be completely banned on boats. It must never be used: if the two ends are not of the same thickness the reef knot will slip, and if it is put under too much strain it becomes impossible to undo. The sheet bend does not suffer from these faults.

The use of the **running clove hitch** must also be understood, as it is of great value when mooring. Make sure that the turns are always made in the same direction as each other: if one wants to undo them easily, the first can be made with a bight in the doubled end of the rope, and the second with the end of the bight.

The **clove hitch** must also be known: two half hitches are made around a solid object instead of around the rope itself. If you think about it, there is nothing very difficult in learning these few knots, and they will serve for almost every imaginable use.

As an extra option, I will add a fifth knot, the **stopper hitch,** which can be

182

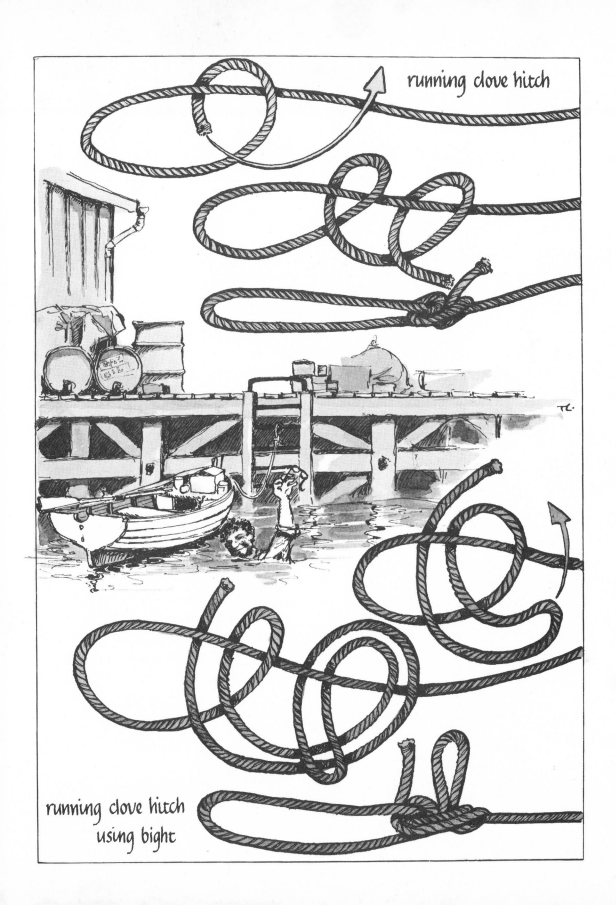

running clove hitch

running clove hitch
using bight

clove hitch

very useful, and which few people know how to make. For example one has two lines made fast to the same cleat, and one wishes to cast off the lower one, but the upper one is under load. One cannot cast it off, and there is too much tension on it for it to be held by hand even for a short time. One must put on a stopper, which allows it to be cast off the cleat without releasing the tension. If you want to adjust the position of your jibsheet lead without allowing the sail to spill wind, here again a stopper is used, which allows the sail to keep pulling and prevents the clew from flogging violently while the position of the lead block is adjusted.

To make a stopper any piece of rope can be used, but it should preferably be flexible. Aboard *Pen Duick VI*, I keep a length of about 3–4 metres which is reserved for the purpose. It is made of 24 mm braided Terylene (Dacron)

184

stopper hitch

185

rope (the warps and sheets of *Pen Duick VI* are of this diameter) from which I have withdrawn the core. It still remains pretty strong, but this gives it great suppleness, which is ideal for a stopper.

The end of the stopper is made fast to a fixed point with a bowline, and the stopper hitch is then made round the line which is under tension. To tie it, a few round turns are wound on back towards where it is made fast, and then carried up in the other direction, winding the stopper in a long spiral the other way from the round turns. Having made four or five turns over about half a metre, the tail is finished off with a clove hitch. The strain is then transferred to the stopper by gently easing out the line which it is holding, allowing the hitch to tighten progressively. Once the stopper has taken the full strain, the line can be cast off altogether.

Finally, I do not think that anyone can be regarded as a sailor who cannot do a little simple sail repairing and splicing. The average yachtsman, sailing a small yacht never far from the services of a sailmaker, can dispense with this knowledge, although he may find it useful. But for ocean cruising it becomes necessary. When the seams finally chafe through one must know how to repair them. One must also know the stitches used to darn a tear: if not, he may finish up with no sails in a fit state to be set. And if one wishes to keep the rigging working well and in good condition, it is indispensable to know the different splices used on fibre and wire ropes.